Cuban Methodism:

The Untold Story of Survival
and Revival

Joe and JoAnn,

Thank you for your many years of faithful
service and support of Cuban Methodism.

Philip Wingeier-Rayo

Philip Wingeier-Rayo, Ph.D.

to order additional copies of this book:
School of Religion,
Pfeiffer University
P.O. Box 960
Misenheimer NC 28109
704/463-1360 ext. 2102
missions@pfeiffer.edu

CUBAN DEMOCRACY:
THE UNTOLD STORY OF SURVIVAL & REVIVAL

copy-editing, layout and design by Stephen Wing

front cover: children in Punta Brava Methodist Church
author & family, page 128: photo by Josefat Photo Studio
back cover: Santa Fe Methodist Church youth group
photo by Diana Wingeier-Rayo

Portions of this book were originally part of a Master's thesis
under advisor Rosemary Radford Ruether at Garrett-Evangelical
Theological Seminary. Portions of Chapter 5 originated as a paper
for a United Methodist Studies class and were later published in
an article co-authored with Paul W. Chilcote, "The Wesleyan
Revival and Methodism in Cuba," *Quarterly Review*, Vol. 17 No. 3
(Fall, 1997), pp. 207-221.

ISBN 0-9650673-3-5

Dolphins & Orchids Publishing
1071 Steeple Run, Lawrenceville GA 30043 USA
www.dolphinsandorchids.com
info@dolphinsandorchids.com

PRINTED ON RECYCLED PAPER

Dedication

To the Cuban people, and sovereign people everywhere who strive for self-determination

To the Cuban church who hosted us and received us as part of the family

To my wife, Diana, without whom our stay in Cuba would not have been possible

To our children, Massiel and Keffren, who embodied the gospel through their love for their Cuban playmates*

To my parents and my brother, Steve, who supported me in this project

*(*see front and back cover photos)*

Table of Contents

Foreword — *Dr. Paul W. Chilcote*   6

Introduction   8

CHAPTER I.   10
Initial Impressions of Cuba

    A 2,000-Kilometer Journey Across Cuba   10
    Biblical Models of Revivalism   14

CHAPTER II.   18
Context of the Cuban Revival:
Collapse of the U.S.S.R.

    Glasnost & Perestroika   18
    Economic Conditions in Cuba   21
    The United States' Embargo of Cuba   26
    Social Conditions in Cuba   28
    Ethical & Philosophical Conditions in Cuba   30

CHAPTER III.   35
Church-State Relations in Socialist Cuba

    An Encounter with Cuban State Security   35
    The Early Years of the Revolution   38
    Dr. Jose Felipe Carneado,
            Minister of Religious Affairs   42
    Castro's Thoughts on Religion   44
    Church-State Relations, 1990-Present   49
    Church Relations Abroad   55

CHAPTER **IV.**   60

Revival within The Methodist Church in Cuba

   Arrival of Methodism in Cuba   60
   Methodism Under the Revolution   64
   The First Rise of the Revival   66
   The Second Rise of the Revival   70
   Conflict & Controversy   77

CHAPTER **V.**   87

**A Comparison: Early Methodism
and Cuban Methodism**

   John Wesley's 18th-Century Revival   87
   The Renewal of Cuban Methodism   95
   Similarities & Differences   104

CHAPTER **VI.**   113

Conclusions & Observations

   Summary   113
   A Mission of Accompaniment   116

Bibliography   123

About the Author   128

Foreword

The Holy Spirit is moving in a powerful way throughout the island of Cuba. Worship there is thrilling. The people of God are radiant. Lives are being transformed. Hopelessness is giving way to hope and a vital sense of purpose and meaning in life. The fruits of the Spirit abound. As is true of many such eruptions of the Spirit in the history and life of the Church, who could have imagined this? Like many renewal movements of the past, the Cuban church is now leading the way to a rediscovered understanding of what life in Christ means.

Like the Wesleyan Revival of 18th-century Britain, this new awakening– albeit in a very different cultural and historical context– bears all the marks of a genuine rediscovery of the essence of the gospel. Cuban Christians are reminding the rest of the Church about the power of God's love as revealed to us in the person of Jesus Christ, the transforming power of faith in him, and the hope which the Spirit engenders in the soul, even in the most difficult of circumstances. The Cuban church has much to teach us all.

Philip Wingeier-Rayo, a former student of whom I am extremely proud, and a former United Methodist missioner to Cuba and other parts of Latin America, has helped to put a "human face" on these amazing developments. He has witnessed firsthand how the promises of God to the children of God are always surprisingly rich packages. He invites you into the journey and the joy.

The faces of the people you will read about in these pages were the faces of a dream. Today, they are the faces of reality. Phil has not only done a marvelous job in reminding us of the story of the amazing phenomenon which is Christianity in Cuba and identifying its characteristic features, but has captured the spirit of the renewal blazing across the island. I highly recommend this book to any who would like to understand more fully this recent story of Christianity in Cuba, to those who long to see the human face of God's mission in this world, and to all who celebrate the inbreaking of God's reign in human history. The story is certain to challenge you personally, to renew your own faith, and to plant an amazing vision in your heart.

> Dr. Paul W. Chilcote
> Professor of Historical Theology &
> Wesleyan Studies
> Asbury Theological Seminary (Florida)

Introduction

Minutes before entering the sanctuary, Rev. Rinaldo Hernández Torres, my host in Cuba, called me into his office to warn me about the style of worship:

"This congregation started a charismatic renewal before I arrived. I was appointed here not to put out the flame, but rather to channel it within Methodist tradition." Trying to prepare me for the shock, he continued, "The worship style will probably be different from that to which you are accustomed."

As I sat down in the pew, I immediately noticed the electric guitar, bass and drum set. The prayer of invocation was barely audible as the congregation, by now "standing room only," were all praying out loud, creating a buzzing sound throughout the large modern sanctuary.

After about twenty minutes, the buzz tapered off and the congregation got up off their knees and stood to face the chancel. The praise band began an hour-long set of enthusiastic praise music with the congregation clapping and singing along. There was no bulletin, no order of worship

Including the sermon and an altar call, the service lasted over two hours. I then understood what Pastor Hernández had meant when he said the worship style was different. In addition to the Sunday service, the church held Bible study, prayer, men's, women's and youth services during the week. The Marianao Methodist Church in Havana was undergoing a charismatic re-

newal, ~~And this was just the tip of the iceberg.~~ *and the movement was spreading throughout the island.* I had arrived in Cuba at a critical time for both the church and soci-
ety. Both were about to undergo radical change forever.

The date was September, 1991 The personal experiences and research for this book
emerged during my six years (1991-1997) as a United Meth-
odist missionary assigned by the General Board of Global Ministries to serve the Methodist Church in Cuba.
After an introductory one-year exchange when I traveled
throughout the island in the fall of 1991, and then accompanied Rev. Hernández on a reciprocal visit to the United
States, my wife Diana and I— along with our two children— became the first missionaries to enter Cuba in
thirty years.

This was a great privilege and a great responsibility.
Upon our arrival in Cuba we found a very tense situation;
the Soviet Union had undergone *perestroika* and collapsed,
resulting in a domino effect for all the Soviet colonies.
In addition to the ensuing material shortages, we found
a Cuba full of uncertainty about the future. All organized
religions began to grow— especially Christianity— as Cubans attempted to answer their existential questions and
fill the void left by the now-discredited communist ideology. This book will examine the survival and subsequent revival of the church within the Socialist revolutionary context.

Philip Wingeier-Rayo

9

CHAPTER I
Initial Impressions of Cuba

A 2,000-Kilometer Journey Across Cuba

Speaking in tongues, "slain in the Spirit," and prophecy in a Methodist Church? This was my initial thought ~~after~~ traveling from Pinar del Rio, the furthest Western province, all the way across the island to Guantanamo in the east.

After experiencing dancing in the aisle during the Methodist Men's Assembly in Pinar del Rio, I traveled 1,000 kilometers, all night long, to Holguin in the back of a 1957 Ford truck. This trip launched a three-month tour of the island utilizing every mode of transportation imaginable— bus, train, taxi, truck, tractor, bicycle, even horseback— to visit remote communities.

Cuba was still off-limits for most Americans, so as I visited isolated communities my presence created a spectacle. In addition to visiting many churches, I also toured a sugar mill, a mine, two quarantine camps for HIV/AIDS patients, state hospitals, schools, and rehabilitation centers for the deaf, blind and mentally challenged.

Perhaps the most interesting visit was to a small town across from the U.S. military base at Guantanamo Bay. The town of Caimanera mysteriously unites Cuba's past, present and future. After being approved by the Central Committee of the Communist Party, I was able to clear the checkpoint and see what used to be a military town for U.S. soldiers in pre-Castro Cuba.

I was told that Caimanera was off-limits because Cubans were tempted to swim across the bay and ask for political asylum at the base. Some had tried, but only a few made it, and most of them drowned. My guide explained that there was a stretch of land dividing the base from Cuban soil that was strewn with mines and lined with barbed wire fences.

The residents of Caimanera had enjoyed a privileged status because of their proximity to temptation. It was the first town to receive color TV sets and new Russian-made cars— supposedly an incentive not to hanker after the material possessions available on the other side. Locals received U.S. television and radio signals repeated by the base. Some Cubans were even allowed to continue to work on the base after President Kennedy broke off diplomatic ties in 1961. They continued to work until they reached retirement age and now receive a pension in dollars from the U.S. military.

I was taken to the town museum, which was organized by the government to display how the Revolution had eradicated the social evils of the Batista dictatorship: gambling, prostitution and social inequality. It also had pictures of U.S. sailors exploiting Cuban women at restaurants and brothels. The museum illustrated a common theme of the Revolution: Cuban nationalism.

Ironically the socialist Revolution was able to nationalize the U.S. oil refineries, but never able to reclaim Guantanamo Bay. Established back in 1902 during the United States' occupation of Cuba, the base is occupied by the U.S. Navy under a unilateral lease for $1.00 a year from the Cuban government.

When Cuba was on the verge of defeating the Spanish and gaining its independence, the United States stationed the U.S.S. *Maine* in the Havana Harbor to protect

U.S. interests. On February 15, 1898, the ship mysteriously exploded and sank, thus provoking President William McKinley to intervene. Less than a year later Teddy Roosevelt's "Rough Riders" defeated the Spanish in what is now known as the Spanish-American War. Cuban historians argue that the explosion was staged to provide a pretext for U.S. intervention.

The United States occupied Cuba for five years. The U.S. Senate passed the Platt Amendment in 1903, granting the U.S. the right to intervene and defend Cuba's independence, and establishing an unlimited lease to the Guantanamo Bay Naval Base.

Nearby the museum a Canadian company was building a hotel overlooking the bay. We climbed to the top story where we looked across and saw the U.S. barracks. As I stood on the roof, taking in the tropical sun and the beautiful Caribbean view, I could not help but reflect on the irony of a U.S. base on Cuban soil. Indeed, Caimanera was a microcosm of Cuba's past, present and future.

Then, in just a 45-minute drive, we returned to today's Cuban reality in Guantanamo city in time to worship at the Methodist Church and experience another charismatic service.

My visit to Guantanamo completed a 2,000-kilometer trip from one end of the island to the other. From the Men's Assembly in Pinar del Rio to the Methodist Church in Guantanamo, I was able to witness firsthand the changing worship style within the changing Cuban context. The sermons were more evangelistic than the messages I heard back home, which emphasized personal ethics and social responsibility. Altar calls or invitations— rarely practiced in the U.S.— follow every sermon in Cuba, with several converts coming forward each time.

During congregational prayer the parishioners pray out loud, thus drowning out the leader and creating a buzzing effect in the sanctuary. This is in contrast to the quiet reverence that I have experienced in the North American church. Cuban services provide an opportunity for churchgoers to share their testimonies, in keeping with the more informal and participatory worship format.

Perhaps the greatest difference is the extraordinary manifestation of the Holy Spirit in Cuban Methodism, such as speaking in tongues, prophecy, healing, discernment of the spirit, and interpretation.

According to my understanding of the Christian faith at that time, I believed that these practices were a way to escape from a difficult reality and seek a vertical relationship with God without regard for those in need around us. The theology that I had studied had taught me to seek out God's power for a collective response to injustice. However, as a missionary trained to appreciate and respect other cultures, I tried not to judge the Cubans, but rather to try to learn about their expression of the faith from the perspective of their context, culture, and socio-economic situation.

As I participated in worship services and engaged in conversation with churchgoers, my awareness of the Cuban situation grew. I understood better the repression felt by the people and their need to seek freedom through worship. Not being Cuban myself, I could not and will never completely be able to put myself in their shoes, but I did learn to be more sensitive to their hardships, particularly those of the Christians.

I heard about the nationalization of church-related schools and clinics as the government assumed control of social services. I listened to stories of personal loss, family separation and frustrated dreams. I also heard stories about the government's attempts to manipulate any genuine effort by the church to help society, publicizing these as political support for Fidel Castro. These experiences helped me better understand the reluctance of the church to be involved in social programs for the general population.

Over time I felt the official discrimination against Christians, as I personally experienced it too. Nevertheless, I continued to question the length and frequency of worship services and the lack of social ministries to meet the needs of those who suffer. More specifically, I asked myself if the charismatic worship and theology of present-day Cuban Methodism was consistent with the Wesleyan tradition.

The question still remains: Is the church growth in Cuba an authentic revival in the Wesleyan tradition or is it merely a form of escapism from harsh socio-economic conditions?

In an effort to resolve this question in my own mind, I turned to the sources of Scripture, tradition, experience, and reason. Specifically I reviewed biblical models of revivalism, the origins of Methodism in 18th century England, and my own experience, and then processed these sources through reason. Realizing that I did not have enough knowledge of early Methodism to answer my own questions, I began reading John Wesley's journals, letters, and treatises. This personal search led me to seminary for two masters' degrees, and eventually to a Ph.D.

After studying the Bible, reading about John Wesley, praying and reflecting, this book emerged as a way to partially answer my questions.

Biblical Models of Revivalism

To better understand the rapid growth of the Cuban church, I researched biblical and theological understandings of revival. In biblical terms, *revival* means "to return to life from amongst the dead."[1] This is similar to *resurrection*, which comes from the verb "to resurrect," meaning "to raise from the dead."[2] These understandings contrast with the words *restore*, *reform* and *renew*, which only deal with the physical condition or form of an inanimate object. To restore is "to bring back to or put back into a former or original state."[3] To reform is "to make better by removal of faults."[4] And to renew is "to restore to freshness or vigor."[5]

The striking difference between *revive* and these other verbs is that, while humans can make plans to restore, reform or renew a physical object, only God is the source of life— so only God can revive. Therefore, our principal error in using the term *revival* is in assuming that human beings can have control over when and where a revival can occur. We can participate in a revival, but ultimately God is its source.

Actually, *revival* does not appear in the Bible in the noun form, but rather only appears as a verb in Hebrew, *haya*— "to enliven, to give life." The prefix "re," which means "again," does not exist in Hebrew. Therefore, in the context of the Old Testament prophets, God is promising to enliven again or to give life again. It is significant that *revive* appears in the Bible as a verb and not as a noun, suggesting that that the revival process is a constant renewing action. Revival is not a static condition, but rather is something that must be continually ongoing or else it is lost.

While in exile, the Israelites longed for a return to the land of Canaan. The cities of their country were in ruins. The people were dispersed and working as slaves in a foreign land. The prophets interpreted this condition as punishment for their unfaithfulness to God. Nevertheless, the prophetic books of the post-exilic period conclude their condemnations with messages of hope prophesying about "new heavens and a new earth." (Isaiah 65:17).

The desire of the Jews was to return to a Davidic kingdom and to reconstruct the temple as a symbol of the strength of Zion. The plans of God, however, were often different from their expectations.

For example, the prophet Amos prophesied the return of "the booth of David" (Haggai 2:9). This indicated a different expectation than that of the people, who wanted the reconstruction of the temple as a prominent and permanent structure. A booth is much more temporary, pointing to the prophet's desire not to return to an institutionalized religio-political structure placing so much emphasis on monarchy. Rather, Amos wanted his people to carry the Law with them in their hearts. The prophet's understanding of *revival* was a new life for God's people, though not necessarily returning to the old institutional religio-political structures.

The prophet Ezekiel also received a revelation of God's plans for the Israelites in the valley of dry bones:

"Then he said to me, 'Prophesy to these bones, and say to them: O dry bones, hear the word of the Lord. Thus says the Lord God to these bones: I will cause breath to enter you, and you shall live. I will lay sinews on you, and will cause flesh to come upon you, and cover you with skin, and put breath in you and you shall live; and you shall know that I am the Lord." (Ezekiel 37:4-6)

Ezekiel is the prophet through whom God reveals the plan to breathe life into dry bones. This is symbolism for a new life for God's people. The spirit or breath of life in Hebrew is *ruah*. This is the same word used in the creation story to refer to giving life to the human: *ha adam* (Genesis 1:27). Only God can give this life and vitality. Even though humans may try to reform, restore or renew our institutions, ultimately it is only God who can give new life (*haya*) and breath (*ruah*).

The Methodist Church in Cuba was not dead, neither

was it in exile, yet it had been severely limited by government restrictions and the exodus of most of its leaders. Many people were questioning whether the church would survive in the face of this extreme adversity. In a sense, these trials purified the church of members who had joined for convenience, and only those remained who were willing to pay the price.

In the late 1960s, a few Methodist pastors began to experience unusual manifestations of the Holy Spirit and started a small renewal movement. People even prayed for a revival, hoping that the church could return to its previous condition. But people did not know what a revival really entailed. The changes made by the Cuban Revolution were permanent and God began to reveal a new vision for the Methodist Church, which began to look less and less like the pre-Castro church established by the missionaries.

Then, in the 1990s, the Methodist Church began to grow in an extraordinary way. While some leaders were striving for renewal of the Methodist Church, God was creating a revival. The next chapter will examine the factors in the Cuban context that created favorable conditions for a revival.

FOOTNOTES

1   *Baker's Dictionary of Theology.* Grand Rapids, MI: Baker Book House, 1960, p.75.
2   *Webster's Intermediate Dictionary.* Springfield, MA: Merriam-Webster Publishers, 1972, p.643.
3   Ibid, p.642.
4   Ibid, p.629.
5   Ibid, p.636.

Chapter II
Context of the Cuban Revival: The Collapse of the U.S.S.R.

Glasnost and Perestroika

My arrival in Cuba in September 1991 as a missionary with the Methodist Church was actually not my first. I had visited two years earlier, before *glasnost* and *perestroika*. The difference was dramatic.

Before, Cubans were enjoying a comfortable standard of living, bordering on abundance. One could walk into any restaurant and enjoy a delicious and inexpensive meal. One could wait at the bus stop for 10 minutes and the bus would arrive on schedule and carry you to your destination. If one was in a hurry, one could flag a taxi, pay a reasonable fare, and arrive on time.

Now, on my second trip, the effects of the collapse of the Soviet Union were apparent. Still accustomed to Soviet subsidies, Cubans complained about food shortages, power outages and poor bus service. The chicken, beef and reliable public transportation of the Soviet years were gone.

After waiting two hours at a bus stop in Havana, I boarded a "standing room only" *camello* (a broken down bus towed by a tractor-trailer rig). During a long and tiresome bus trip, I overheard a passenger sharing news from her doctor's appointment. She said that the physician

18

had put her on a low-cholesterol diet with no eggs. She laughed as she told her friend, "If I don't eat eggs, what does he expect me to eat?"

The sudden cessation of favorable trade agreements with Eastern Europe created a devastating economic crisis in Cuba. The Soviet Union had established favorable economic trade agreements beneficial to Cuba in the early 1960s. This made Cuba dependent upon the Soviet Union in the areas of exports, imports, trading terms, trade partner concentration, energy, transportation and external indebtedness.[6] These agreements and subsidies allowed Cuba to be relatively stable and prosperous, especially compared to neighboring Latin American countries, until the early 1990s.

This relationship began to change when Soviet President Mikhail Gorbachev opened the door for *glasnost* and *perestroika* in the Soviet Union in the mid-1980s. Fidel Castro and the leadership of the Cuban government were aware of these changes, and made attempts to isolate the island. For example, certain Soviet publications such as *Sputnik*, once frequently found on Cuban news stands, were banned from Cuba in 1991. Castro was opposed to the Soviet process of *glasnost* and *perestroika* and hoped to limit its influence on Cuba.[7]

In response to the Soviet measures, the Cuban Communist Party called for *"Rectificacion"* at their 1986 Congress. This internal reform process reacted against *glasnost* and *perestroika* by discontinuing earlier experiments with the free market system, such as the farmers' market, and returning to traditional Marxism-Leninism.[8] The congress also reaffirmed the Party's commitment to hardline communism, asking the people to sacrifice for the common good and emphasizing moral obligation as incentive to greater production.[9]

In spite of the party's efforts to isolate Cuba, its dependent trade relationship with the Soviet Union and Eastern Europe would eventually affect Cuba in a very direct way. In 1989, 70 percent of Cuba's foreign trade was with the former Soviet Union, and 80 percent of all foreign trade was with Eastern bloc countries.[10] Eighty percent of Cuba's sugar production went to the Soviet Union, along with 40 percent of its citrus.[11] Cuba was also receiving as much as five to seven billion dollars a year in aid. The U.S. State Department breaks this down to $4.3 billion dollars of economic aid and $1.5 billion in military aid.[12] There were 15,000 Soviet troops in Cuba in 1989.[13] Also, Cuba was approximately 30 billion dollars in debt to the Soviet Union.[14] Cuba received 13 million tons of oil a year, or 270 barrels a day, about 95 percent of Cuba's supply, from the former superpower.[15]

This heavy dependency left Cuba completely vulnerable to the swift changes that were about to unfold in the world. In November of 1989 the Berlin Wall fell, thus uniting the People's Democratic Republic of Germany with West Germany. In 1990 the Soviet Union began to renege on its trade agreements with Cuba. On the verge of financial crisis, Fidel Castro announced in his speech on the anniversary of the Bay of Pigs in April 1990 that the country would begin a *"periódo especial en tiempo de paz"* (special period in peacetime).[16]

Later on this term would become a catch-all excuse for any problems or shortages. Often *"periódo especial"* would be the butt of Cuban jokes. For example, when asked how to say *"periódo especial"* in French, a Cuban replied *"ique escasez!"* (what scarcity!) The government was aware of the shortages that were to come and this announcement sought to prepare the people psychologically for greater sacrifice.

In August 1991 the *coup d'etat* in the former Soviet Union began the official disbanding of Soviet states into what would later become independent sovereign nations.[17] As a result, the now nonexistent Soviet Union unilaterally broke its trade agreements with Cuba. Between 1989 and 1992 Cuba received 60 percent fewer imports from abroad and due to the shortage of raw materials and energy had 40 percent less production.[18]

The new Russian republic ended all subsidies to Cuba and negotiated a new agreement in November 1992, which demanded that all future trade be at current world prices.[19] Some of the independent Soviet states did the same, and the loss of imports was dramatic, forcing the Cuban economy into a tailspin. Unable to establish new trade partners with such short notice, Cuba faced great scarcities in major commodities such as food, energy, raw materials and medicines.

Economic Conditions in Cuba

Although most goods were already rationed in Cuba, the portions were further reduced.[20] For instance, in 1989 Cuba received 13 million tons of oil from the Soviet Union, but by 1992 the economy was running on 5 million tons from different sources.[21] This led to gasoline rations of only 20 liters a month for private automobiles and less fuel available for public transportation. Most electricity in Cuba was generated from petroleum-burning plants, thus causing increasingly longer power outages.

The lack of fuel led to a 40 percent reduction of transportation over two years.[22] Since the majority of people in Cuba do not own cars, they are highly dependent on a public transportation system. During my first visit to Cuba in July and August of 1989, I was able to travel all over Havana and out to the province of Las Villas on a relatively efficient public transportation system. The urban buses ran every ten minutes and one could reach any part of Havana on a combination of routes.

However, by my next visit in the fall of 1991, I found a nearly paralyzed public transportation system. Fuel shortages had forced the Ministry of Transportation to cut back buses on all routes, and some routes were canceled altogether. People waited as long as four hours between buses, and often children and elderly were trampled when the long line of desperate commuters converged on the bus. Train tickets were scarce and opportunists scalped them on the "black market" for outrageous prices.

During this second visit, the leadership of the church designed a three-month itinerary for me to get to know the reality of the church and the country from *occidente a orient* (west to east). I traveled across Cuban provinces and found bus and train terminals crowded with people waiting in long lines to secure tickets to their destinations. Inter-provincial bus routes were cut back from an efficient hourly service to only two buses per day. For example, I remember missing the 5:00 a.m. bus from Niquero to Pilon in eastern Cuba (which by car is only a two-hour trip), and having to wait in the terminal for the 5:00 p.m. bus.

Taxis became less and less available for the public, being officially reserved for hospital and funeral service. Yet taxi drivers used their state-owned vehicles to advantage by spending their personal gasoline rations to start an off-hours taxi service at the "black market" rate. The few Cubans that owned private automobiles could either try to do the same or just park their cars in favor of bicycles. Those who had access to dollars could buy gasoline at a chain of tourist gas stations called CUPET that began in the early 1990s and later became a joint venture between Cuba and Mexico.

In 1991 the government foresaw these shortages and

imported a million Chinese bicycles, which initially led to a rash of accidents. The same year the Ministry of Transportation announced the organization of a new police force, affectionately nicknamed *amarillos* because of their yellow uniforms, whose responsibility it was to flag down state vehicles and board would-be travelers going in the same direction.

In the late 1990s the government even experimented with private transportation, allowing entrepreneurs to install benches in truck beds and start their own "bus" routes. Early entrepreneurs were constantly being fined or hassled, as local government officials would contend with national policymakers over whether it was legal to have such a profitable business. Prevented by the U.S. embargo from turning to their northern neighbor for car parts and fossil fuels, ordinary Cubans suffered the most through everyday inconveniences.

The makeshift transportation solutions were quite dangerous. On our way into Havana, we often saw young people riding their bikes long distances and holding on to the backs of trucks or buses to rest their legs. In addition to the rise in bicycle accidents, the trucks and *camellos* were ill-suited for public transportion. As car parts were scarce and vehicles in disrepair, accidents became commonplace. On several occasions we saw serious accidents and a dear friend of ours died when a truck full of passengers overturned on the highway.

Lacking electricity and raw materials, many of the factories were forced to close or slow production. Food confection and pharmaceuticals, for example, depended on raw materials from Eastern Europe to continue production. When the trade agreements were discontinued those industries were paralyzed until such materials could be obtained in other markets. However, the tightening of the U.S. embargo with the passage of the Cuban

A Cuban Bodega (corner store)

Democracy Act restricted Cuba's ability to obtain food and medicines from other countries.

All of this resulted in unemployment and half-time positions. In spite of efforts by the Cuban government to maintain people on the payroll, unemployment was discouraging for a proud and hard working population. Not only did these partial factory closings hurt national production, they also affected people's self-esteem as productive members of society.

In addition to the cut-off of food imports, the fuel shortage hurt agricultural production and distribution. Sugar production dropped from seven million tons in the 1991-92 harvest to four million tons in 1993-94.[23] Although people were entitled to certain quantities of food according to their ration cards, the produce simply was not available. The Cuban Methodist Church recognized these concerns in a June 1993 pastoral letter:

"We are sensitized to the situation of our people's diet. The basic staples of the family basket have been reduced to minimum quantities and many products have been reserved for children, and no longer arrive for the adult population. Agricultural production is insufficient and unstable. Fruits and vegetables are almost out of reach for the consumers, especially in the large cities."[24]

Although the Cuban Revolution was able to make astounding achievements in the area of health care during its first three decades, the 1990s brought devastating blows to the quality of health care available to the population. Even though the infrastructure of hospitals, nurses and doctors was still in place, the shortage of medical supplies was critical. Patients were effectively diagnosed by their physicians, but oftentimes unable to fulfill the most basic prescriptions.

The American Association for World Health recognized that of the 1,297 medications available in Cuba in 1991, only 889 of these same medicines were still available by 1997.[25] The pharmacies could not stock enough medicines to meet demands and the hospitals reserved their supplies for the most urgent cases. Cuba has an excellent pharmaceutical industry that, with the aid of former Soviet bloc countries, was able to produce much of its own medicines. However, after the fall of the Berlin Wall, Cuban production was limited to medicines for which all the raw materials were available in Cuba. The U.S. embargo also made it difficult for the Ministry of Public Health to obtain necessary ingredients. With limited hard currency, the Cuban authorities were forced to purchase medical supplies from European pharmaceutical companies with higher transportation costs.[26]

The food shortage and ensuing vitamin deficiencies also affected health conditions. The American Association for World Health estimated that the daily caloric intake dropped 33 percent from 1989 to 1993.[27] Many illnesses related to malnutrition and low immunity defenses began to emerge during the "special period." For example, in 1992 a rare illness reached epidemic proportions in Cuba. Optic neurosis or *neuritis*, as it is called in Cuba, is caused by a lack of protein in the diet and certain toxins in the bloodstream and produces nerve damage, strained eyesight, pain in the joints and lethargy. Again, the withdrawal of Soviet aid, combined with a tightening U.S. embargo, created worsening health conditions and diet in Cuba.

Prior to the fall of the Berlin Wall, Cubans were able to buy certain clothes and shoes in their own currency, (the peso) ~~the Cuban peso~~, according to a scheduled ration. Additional clothes were available on the "black market" at a slightly higher cost. However, with the withdrawal of Soviet aid, these supplies became extremely scarce. Although one was entitled to these items through one's ration card, the merchandise simply was not in stock. The only place to acquire these goods was in the "dollar stores" or ~~on the "black market."~~ buy them contraband on the street.

The dollar stores, called *tiendas diplomaticas*, are a chain of government-run outlet stores with merchandise from capitalist countries. U.S. brand names are readily available through U.S. subsidiary companies via Panama. Originally the stores were off-limits to Cubans unless accompanied by a foreigner, but in 1993 the possession of U.S. dollars was de-penalized and Cubans fortunate enough to possess dollars are now free to shop there. The "black market" was everyone involved in buying and selling goods on the street. Opportunists took advantage of their access to merchandise and ~~overpriced~~ resell it for the majority of the population.

The United States' Embargo of Cuba

Just as Cuba faced scarcities from the collapse of the socialist bloc, Cuban-Americans lobbied the U.S. government for a tougher foreign policy toward Cuba. In 1992

Congressman Robert Torrecelli (D-NJ), representing a district with a large Cuban-American constituency, sponsored the Cuban Democracy Act.

Signed by President George Bush on October 23, 1992, the law prohibited foreign ships that had traded with Cuba from entering U.S. ports and denied aid and debt reduction to any nation that continued to trade with Cuba. In addition, the law prohibited foreign-based subsidiaries of U.S. companies from trading with Cuba and banned Cuban-Americans from sending cash remittances to their families. Invoking the ancient Trading with the Enemy Act, the law rescinded President Carter's permission for U.S. citizens to travel and spend U.S. dollars in Cuba.[28]

This clause affected us personally since we were already in Cuba under the auspicies of the General Board of Global Ministries of the United Methodist Church. While we tried to live as simply as possible to be in solidarity with the people, we obviously needed U.S. dollars to survive— to buy supplies not available to us through the ration system.

We were permitted to stay in Cuba in relative obscurity until a Cuban-American organization called *Hermanos al Rescate* (Brothers to the Rescue) provoked an international incident. Having flown over Cuban territory and dropped anti-government leaflets in the past, three planes ventured into Cuban airspace on February 26, 1996. The Cuban Air Force made radio contact with the pilots and repeatedly warned them to retreat. Under a direct order from President Castro the Cuban Air Force shot down two planes over Cuban waters, killing four members of *Hermanos al Rescate.*

At the time we were in Atlanta visiting a supporting church and our children were in Cuba. We were alarmed by rumors that all flights to Cuba would be suspended indefinitely. Backed by the prayers of our supporting church, we traveled back to Cuba via Mexico and were safely reunited with our children. Nevertheless, diplomatic relations between Cuba and the United States were so tense that the mission board asked us not to leave Cuba again until the end of our term of service. This was very disappointing since we had a family reunion scheduled that summer in Atlanta with tickets to attend the 1996 Olympic Games. Nevertheless, we realized the seriousness of the situation and remained in Cuba.

In response to the international incident, President Clinton tightened the screws further on March 12, 1996, by signing the Cuban Liberty and Democratic Solidarity Act, better known as the Helms-Burton Act. While opening a window for civil exchange between non-governmental and humanitarian groups, the law granted authority to the U.S. Department of Treasury to fine foreign companies who trade with Cuba and also deny U.S. entry to their employees. Canada and England, among other U.S. allies, criticized this law and accused the United States of imposing its foreign policy on sovereign nations. The changes in foreign policy made it even more difficult for Cuba to find trade partners, thus exacerbating the already critical economic conditions.[29]

Social Conditions in Cuba

The effect of the tightening embargo was more hardship for Cubans. People worked and scrounged to meet their daily needs, often just making enough money to put food on the table that day. The majority were forced to go without basic supplies. Parents faced the dilemmas of choosing between purchasing food or a light bulb for their house, shoes or a backpack for their children, between repairing the refrigerator or buying medicine for their children. Items such as toilet paper, meat, and medi-

* for example a home and away baseball series between the Baltimore Orioles and the Cuban national team.

cine became luxuries for the average Cuban. This was a bitter pill to swallow after Soviet subsidies had afforded them these amenities at reasonable prices for the past three decades under the ration system.

The scarcities had a psychosomatic effect, resulting in anxiety and depression. Struggling to cope, many Cubans were on the verge of nervous breakdown leading to a higher incidence of emotional disturbances and suicide: "The indexes of suicide, divorce and abortion grow," observed a 1997 report of the American Association for World Health. "We again see the mentally ill on the street."[30]

The frustration that resulted from this rapid economic decline was expressed through a greater level of violence in society. These concerns were raised in a pastoral letter written by the Conference of Catholic Bishops in 1993:

"The fathers, mothers, priests, educators, agents of the public order and authorities feel uneasy about the growth of delinquency: robberies, assaults, growth of prostitution and violence for generally disproportionate causes. This behavior is many times the manifestation of a repressed aggression that generates personal insecurity in the street and even at home. The scarcity of the most elemental materials: food, medicine, transportation, electricity, etc. favor a tense environment which, on occasions, makes the usual peaceful and cordial Cuban behavior disappear."[31]

Thus, there was a direct correlation between the material scarcity and the dramatic increase of psychosomatic illnesses.

Following the path of least resistance, the population began to seek a livelihood elsewhere– both inside and outside Cuba.[32] Migration, both from the interior of the country to the cities and an exodus abroad, created a so-

Some moved in search of work within Cuba to larger cities and tourist areas creating a

Others went to great lengths to immigrate abroad to

cial problem through the separation of families. When-
ever one is forced to risk one's life and divide the family
there is great anxiety, as a 1994 article in the Canadian
magazine *Maclean's* illustrates:

"For three young brothers in Havana, who were in-
specting their homemade raft before setting off for
Florida, even the prospect of life in a refugee camp held
more promise than Cuba's harsh realities. 'There is nothing left for me here,' said Oxaini Bascaro, 18. 'There are
no jobs, there is not enough food.' His sister, Osuni Avilez,
came to the beach for an emotional farewell. 'I don't want
to see them go, but they say they want freedom to make a
better way of life,' she said. 'All I can do is pray that they
will make it there, because we hear of so many people
who have perished at sea.'"[33]

In addition to emigration, thousands of people
moved within Cuba to Havana or tourist areas to look for
jobs.[34] This contributed to social dislocation as many
people found themselves adapting to unfamiliar urban
environments.

Ethical and Philosophical Conditions in Cuba

The economic crisis also translated into an ideological crisis. People who had been supportive of the Communist regime began to doubt the state ideology as personal sacrifices became too great. Young people who had
been educated in government schools had been taught
that socialism was the hope of the world and that the Soviet Union was their model nation. When the Soviet
Union dissolved and socialism entered a crisis, these
young people questioned governmental ideology and
looked for faith elsewhere.

As Shawn Malone of Georgetown University's Center for Latin American Studies put it, "Cuba's 'Special Period in Time of Peace,' the government's designation for

the post-Cold War crisis period, has generated not only economic questions but also spiritual and philosophical ones, and many Cubans have looked to the churches for answers to multiple concerns."[35]

The ideological slogans and encouragement of Fidel were no longer enough to motivate people to trust the government. Economic instability, just as the designers of the U.S. embargo intended, contributed to growing disapproval of the Castro regime.

The economic crisis also contributed to a general state of existential crisis and uncertainty about the future. The deterioration of conditions was occurring so quickly that people became very anxious. A combination of financial demands at home, the sacrifice involved with studying, and the lack of future incentives in the workplace contributed to a growing high school dropout rate. Why study if thieves make more money on the "black market" than doctors, engineers and lawyers? Truancy became a problem because young people lost faith in the usefulness of an education. Changes occurred so quickly that the population began to feel the instability of the infrastructure.

The influences of Soviet-style Marxism-Leninism had placed great emphasis on materialist philosophy.[36] This understanding of the universe encourages the use of logic and reason over one's feelings. The socialist revolution attempted to satisfy the population's physical needs— education, health care and housing— while placing little emphasis on spiritual and emotional needs.

The revolutionary government attempted to create *el nuevo hombre* ("the new man"), who would be completely selfless in his work for the well-being of society while delaying self-gratification. After several years of working toward the betterment of society without personal gain, and now an economic crisis requiring still greater sacrifices, even the most hardcore government support-ers began to doubt the viability of state ideology. The moral values of the country entered a downward spiral.

The communist system holds the ideal that the state belongs to all. Thus long-deprived workers felt at liberty to help themselves to state property. This was not legal, but need was so great and workers so underpaid that it became acceptable and rarely punished. In Cuban slang the word *resolver* (to resolve) became synonymous with "to steal"– the widespread practice of taking from one's employer what one needed to survive.

Sexual promiscuity became even more predominant, especially among adolescents. Prostitution, illegal since the early 1960s, took a unique Cuban form and became a major social problem, especially with adolescent girls. Be-fore the de-penalization of the dollar, *jiniteras* ("women jockeys") traded sexual favors with foreigners in ex-change for much-needed hygiene products from the dol-lar store. This changed slightly after July 1993 when the U.S. dollar was legalized by the state. Government offi-cials are accused of looking the other way in order to at-tract much-needed foreign tourists for a type of sex tour-ism.

Although the philosophy of cultural relativism makes ethical values contextual, the crisis eroded moral-ity according to Cuban standards. Oppressive state poli-cies demanding allegiance to the government forced people to publicly affirm the regime, while privately criti-cizing it, created a *"doble cara"* (double-faced) phenom-enon. People became increasingly more comfortable not telling the truth when their personal safety was at risk. Fear contributed to a lip service in support of the Castro government and repercussions for society at large. This phenomenon was acknowledged as a social problem by the Communist Party Congress in 1991.[37]

In summary, the dependent relationship that Cuba had with Eastern Europe, particularly the Soviet Union, made its collapse particularly devastating for the Cuban economy. The economic crisis in Cuba generated many social problems, such as a transportation shortage, power outages, unemployment, food scarcities and lack of medicine. These shortages created a tense environment in society where people lived in a state of high anxiety over meeting their basic needs. This generated increasing emotional illnesses, violence, and suicide. Migration, both national and international, was the result of people seeking better-paying jobs. This caused family separation and social dislocation. Moral and ethical values also were affected as people struggled to survive.

As intended, the Cuban Democracy Act and the Helms-Burton Act exacerbated the economic and social crisis, thus eroding support for the Castro government. The crisis also created a lack of trust in existing ideologies and led to a general existential search for the truth. And specifically for the subject of this book, the events of the late 1980s and early 1990s created favorable conditions for a spiritual revival.

FOOTNOTES

6   Carmelo Mesa-Lago, *The Economy of Socialist Cuba*, Albuquerque: University of New Mexico Press, 1981.

7   J. Richard Planas, "The Impact of Soviet Reforms on Cuban Socialism," *Conflict and Change in Cuba.* Enrique A. Baloyra and James A. Morris (eds.), Albuquerque: New Mexico Press, p.248.

8   Although later in 1995 the farmers' market was reinstated to address the food shortages in urban areas.

9   Background Notes. U.S. State Department, 1990, p.5.

10   Background Notes. U.S. State Department, 1993, p.7.

11   Ibid.

12   Background Notes. U.S. State Department, 1990, p.5.

13   Background Notes. U.S. State Department, 1993, p.4.

14   U.S. congressional hearing, statement by Jiri Valenta,

Institute of Soviet and East European Studies, University of Miami.

15 Background Notes. U.S. State Department, 1990, p.4.

16 U.S. congressional hearing, "Cuba in a Changing World: The United States-Soviet-Cuba Triangle," April 30, Bernard Aronson, Assistant Secretary of State for Latin America. July 11 and 31, 1991, iii, p.231.

17 J. Richard Planas, "The Impact of Soviet Reforms on Cuban Socialism," p.256.

18 Background Notes. U.S. State Department, 1993, p.7.

19 Ibid, p.4.

20 Background Notes. U.S. State Department, 1990, p.5.

21 Background Notes. U.S. State Department, 1993, p.7.

22 Ibid.

23 Andrew Bilski, "Damning the Flood," *Maclean's*, Vol.107, No. 35, August 29, 1994, p.18(2).

24 *La Iglesia Metodista en Cuba, "Mensaje de la Conferencia Annual,"* June 1993.

25 "The Impact of the U.S. Embargo on Health and Nutrition in Cuba," Report from the American Association for World Health, March 1997.

26 Ibid.

27 Ibid.

28 www.Cubabloqueo.cu/leyes/cda.pdf

29 www.historyofcuba. com/history/funfacts/embargo.htm

30 American Association for World Health, March 1997. My translation.

31 *"El Amor todo lo Espera,"* message from the Conference of Catholic Bishops of Cuba, September 1993, *La Voz de La Iglesia en Cuba*, Mexico: Buena Prensa, S.A., 1995, p.408. My translation.

32 Philip Wingeier-Rayo, "One Who Stayed," *New World Outlook*, Jan-Feb, 1995, p.38.

33 Bilski, p.34.

34 Larry Rohter, "Cuba's unwanted refugees," *New York Times*, Vol.147, No.293, Oct. 20, 1997, p.A6.

35 Shawn T. Malone, "Conflict, Coexistence, and Cooperation: Church-State Relations in Cuba," Washington: Georgetown University, Center for Latin American Studies, School of Foreign Service, August, 1996, p.8.

36 Emphasized by Rev. Emilio Gonzalez in an interview in Zolfo Springs, Florida, March 21, 1998.

37 *"El Amor todo lo Espera,"* p.410.

Chapter III
Church-State Relations
in Socialist Cuba

Our first Christmas in Cuba. (Photo: auto-timer.)

An Encounter with Cuban State Security

Spending my first Christmas in Cuba with my Nicaraguan wife and children was like being a fish out of water. We were the only home in the whole town that had Christmas decorations and a tree. I recorded this in my diary:

"We had an awkward, but still wonderful Christmas—our first in Cuba! We exchanged gifts at midnight on

Christmas eve and had a traditional Nicaraguan meal with a chicken roast. It was awkward because we were the only family on the block with a Christmas tree and music."

Christmas is not a holiday in Cuba and Christmas trees were illegal in public places until Fidel lifted the prohibition in 1998. Following my wife's Nicaraguan custom, we had our celebration on Christmas eve with a roasted hen.

Getting the hen was another adventure. After we had become friends with the sales clerk at the corner store, he bashfully asked my wife for a pair of shoes, saying, "My brother is getting married on Saturday, and I have no shoes for the wedding." Unable to have dollars or shop

The author plucking the infamous hen (photo: Diana Wingeier-Rayo)

at the *tienda diplomatica* (dollar store), he asked us to buy the shoes in exchange for Cuban pesos. My wife agreed to buy him the shoes, but rejected any remuneration, seeing the gift a part of our mission work.

A few days before Christmas the clerk knocked on the door with a live hen. While we had requested nothing in exchange, the hen seemed like a sincere gesture of gratitude, and besides, it was just in time for Christmas dinner.

Just after the New Year, we were meeting with the bishop to plan some events when the phone rang. Dr. José Felipe Carneado, Minister of Religious Affairs, was on the line informing the bishop that his missionaries were dealing on the "black market"! The bishop listened politely, although sure that there must be some mistake. He hung up the phone and explained that we must be very careful, since we were the first missionaries entering in Cuba and the government had assigned a spy to us 24 hours a day.

We tried to recall who could have been listening or observing our conversation, and then it dawned on us. The sales clerk from the store had been a government agent all the time! We learned our lesson to be careful what we said and did, and with whom.

Bishop Ajo had developed a strong enough relationship with Carneado to overcome minor misunderstandings. Ajo had stayed in Cuba after spending two years and eight months as an inmate of the *Unidades Militares de Ayuda a la Produccion* (Military Units to Aid Production, or U.M.A.P.), and had earned respect as a sympathizer of the Cuban Revolution. It was largely due to this trusting relationship that the government had permitted the Methodist Church to experiment with bringing the first missionary of any denomination into Cuba under the Castro regime.

The warming of church-state relations in the late 1980s and early '90s is another factor contributing to Cuba's spiritual revival. Faced with dire economic conditions, eroding support from Eastern Europe, and a tightening U.S. embargo, the Cuban government saw improving church-state relations as a gesture of good faith toward the West. The churches, particularly those denominations with large North American partner churches, were also seen both as an avenue for influencing public opinion and a source of humanitarian aid. At the same time, the churches in Cuba began to enjoy greater religious freedom and privileges.

Although I will deal with church-state relations in general, the experience of the Roman Catholic Church is quite different from that of the Protestants, and the Methodist Church in particular.

The Early Years of the Revolution

The Cuban people have always been religious. At the triumph of the Revolution in 1959, the country represented a rainbow of religious beliefs ranging from Afro-Cuban religions to Judaism. The largest sector belonged to the Afro-Cuban religion of Santeria, which is a syncretism of Roman Catholicism with worship of African deities. Although traditionally the population has been nominally Roman Catholic, colonial Cuba was poorly evangelized; most of its churchgoers have been upper and middle class urban *criollos* (Cuban-born descendents of Spain).[38] By the time of the Revolution the Protestants were a small, yet well-organized sector of the population.

Immediately following the triumph of the Revolution the overwhelming majority of the population, church-going or not, was supportive of the change. However, this blanket support was short-lived. On the eve of the Bay of Pigs invasion on April 17, 1961, Fidel Castro declared the Revolution to be socialist in character. Many religious leaders immediately began to fear for the future of the church. In June of that same year the government nationalized all private schools and hospitals under the Ministries of Education and Public Health.[39]

Although these institutions were to be used for the same purpose as before, free of charge, for the general population, religious leaders took offense. This began a period of heightened tensions between church and state. Also, after efforts failed to retain diplomatic relations with the U.S., Cuba entered a deepening economic, political and military relationship with the Soviet Union, thus making itself susceptible to Marxist ideology.

Unfortunate incidents, ideological differences, and misunderstandings deepened the state's mistrust of the church. Three Catholic priests were captured in the paramilitary invasion of returned exiles popularly known as the Bay of Pigs.[40] The government responded by deporting 132 Catholic priests.[41] Many of these priests were from Spain and were supporters of Franco, who had fought against the communists in the bloody Spanish civil war.[42] Also, the Roman Catholic Church had been traditionally allied with the upper and middle classes and continued to respond to the interests of this sector, even as it operated in exile.[43] Of the 800 priests in pre-revolutionary Cuba, expulsions and voluntary departures depleted 75 percent.[44]

In the case of the Protestant church, some Cuban leaders were influenced ideologically by their North American mentors in favor of capitalism and against socialism.[45] The United States was living the cold war against the Soviet Union and McCarthyism had created a blacklist for anyone remotely associated with the communist party or ideology. The close association between the Cuban and North American churches had created a pro-American bias, which became a stigma after the Revolution. The Cuban church began to search for its own place in the new revolutionary context, as described by Carlos Camps Cruell:

"The sowing of the gospel by the missionary was realized in a society conformed to a dependent capitalist mode of production with the arrival of North American hegemonic expansion. We carry out the analysis of its implications in a different reality, socialist, in the midst of a hostile and antagonistic life experience which exemplifies the relations between our two countries."[46]

Following the rupture of diplomatic relations between the two countries in January 1961, the North American missionaries were recalled by their respective mission boards. This paved the way for several key leaders to depart as well. In the case of the Methodist Church of Cuba, at that time still legally under the auspices of the Florida episcopal area, 42 of 51 Cuban pastors would eventually emigrate.[47] The Protestant church had inherited an anti-communism bent, and was struggling to survive in a new nationalistic society.

In 1965 the Cuban government began to force pastors to participate in the U.M.A.P. program— the most serious human rights offense committed by the government against the church. Church leaders and pastors were forcibly recruited to participate in these work brigades, along with homosexuals, thieves and social misfits.[48] Theoretically the government was attempting to change their ideological perspective, but in reality they were sent to work camps in the province of Camaguey to cut sugar cane under harsh conditions. Cardinal Jaime Ortega and former Methodist Bishop Joel Ajo were two inmates placed in the same unit.[49]

Some pastors saw the imprisonment as a chance to show the authorities that Christians had noble qualities, and took advantage of opportunities to counsel other inmates and become squad leaders. These pastors developed a positive attitude toward their role in a socialist society, and after their release managed to reconcile themselves to their internment. Other pastors were unable to overcome the bitterness of captivity and upon release sought to flee the country. After two years and eight months the government closed the U.M.A.P. due to domestic and international pressure, later admitting that it was a mistake.[50]

Although the U.M.A.P. was the most blatant policy of persecution against Christians, there was also a blanket discrimination against churchgoers that discouraged religious affiliation. College students who wanted to study in certain fields, such as psychology, education, journalism, or any other "influential careers" were rejected on the basis of religious affiliation.[51] Career advancement, promotions and certain administrative positions were closed to Christians. Children were asked in school if they were believers, and if they said yes, were publicly chastised and this information was placed in their report cards.

Shawn Malone of the Georgetown Center for Latin American Studies explains: "Individual clergy were persecuted, religious services were obstructed or disrupted, church property was vandalized, educational and occupational access for believers was restricted, and, for a brief period in the 1960s, 'reeducation camps' grouped priests with prostitutes, criminals, and other 'anti-social elements.'"[52]

These methods, along with advancement incentives for those who gave their loyalty to the Revolution, were generally effective. Formerly large congregations dwindled down to 20 or 30 people.[53] Many Christians left the church or left the country entirely. To remain a Christian during the early years of the Revolution involved making a significant sacrifice.

Although the 1960s was indeed a very conflictive decade for church-state relations in Cuba, the 1970s would bring the realization that neither the church nor the state was going to disappear anytime soon. Following the Cuban missile crisis in October 1962, the United States agreed not to attack in exchange for the removal of nuclear weapons. So the Cuban Revolution was protected in favor of reducing the greater geo-political danger of a nuclear war. The Revolution had won and would stay in power, but a remnant of clergy and laity had the resolve to stay, so both sides had to learn to co-exist.

Dr. José Felipe Carneado: Minister of Religious Affairs

A central figure in Cuban church-state relations was Dr. José Felipe Carneado (1915-1993). A leader in the student movement and Communist Party since the 1930s, Dr. Carneado was a Cuban patriot who, although a communist and nationalist, was very respectful of religion. He was appointed by Fidel to be in charge of religious affairs in 1961, and this evolved into a cabinet-level position in 1966 when the Office of Religious Affairs of the Central Committee of the Communist Party was officially opened.[54]

Dr. Carneado was not a believer himself, although he saw where Christianity and socialism could cooperate. "There is no essential incompatibility between well-understood religious criteria and the disposition to work together on a useful social project for society," he wrote.[55] Certainly not enamored of religious beliefs or practices himself, Carneado was at least respectful.[56] Although he was under obligation to carry out the party line, he listened to the issues raised by religious leaders and was in

Dr. Jose Felipe Carneado.

a position to influence party policy over time. He said of his position:

"I have felt the backing of the Party leadership. I have worked to discover the fundamental thought of the revolutionary leadership, particularly that of Fidel. That is why it would be arrogant on my part to attribute to myself what in reality is the party. I am in reality a representative because I only reflect this policy."[57]

For three decades Carneado was a voice in the Cuban cabinet standing up for a respectful church-state policy. Carneado was an effective liaison in church-state relations until his death in March 1993.

Fidel Castro's Thoughts on Religion

As Dr. Carneado was subject to the authority of Fidel Castro, it is essential to outline several key experiences that influenced the Cuban president's understanding of religion. Born in eastern Cuba to Roman Catholic parents, Fidel was baptized relatively late, at the age of five, after being derogatorily called a "Jew."[58] Beginning his elementary education at a Roman Catholic boarding school operated by the Brothers of La Salle in Santiago de Cuba, he transferred in the fifth grade to a prestigious Jesuit school, Colegio de Dolores.[59]

Following his second year of high school, by his own choice he transferred to an upper-class Jesuit school in Havana called Colegio de Belen.[60] He graduated from high school in 1945 and entered the law department at the Universidad de La Habana.[61] Here Castro became very active in the student movement and applied his sound religious education toward participation in politics.

Shortly after Castro graduated from the university with a law degree, General Fulgencio Batista executed a *coup d'etat* in March 10, 1952, and became the dictator of Cuba. Castro observed that it would be impossible to achieve the social changes that he desired through civil means, so he plotted an armed insurrection.[62] He trained a group of friends and former classmates and orchestrated an attack on the Moncada military armory in Santiago on July 26, 1956. This attack failed miserably, and both Fidel and his brother Raul Castro were captured, but it alerted the population to the existence of a movement to overthrow Batista. Castro was imprisoned for 14 months until he was exiled to Mexico by presidential pardon.

Never a quitter, he re-organized his troops and trained them for another insurrection in Cuba. While in Mexico, Fidel befriended Ernesto Guevara, an Argentinean doctor who became a beloved revolutionary hero affectionately known as *"El Che."* On December 4, 1957, Castro's troops disembarked in Cuba's Oriente province, where they began a two-year insurrection that finally caused

Batista to flee Cuba on January 1, 1959.

During the insurrection, students, labor unions and peasants organized a resistance movement against the dictatorship. One prominent participant in the Revolution was Frank Pais, son of a Baptist pastor, choir boy and Sunday school teacher, and an activist whose courage and faith greatly impressed Castro. As the president of the student movement in Santiago de Cuba, Pais coordinated a protest to distract the National Army during Castro's secret return from exile aboard the yacht *Granma*. Pais was eventually killed when the army dispersed a demonstration in the streets of Santiago and shot him on the street. He is remembered as a beloved hero of the Revolution.

Castro's troops created a liberated zone in Cuba's eastern mountains where he introduced social programs such as literacy classes and free health care. Priests volunteered to teach classes and even fought with Castro's troops. In addition, the peasants and many of his guerrilla soldiers were believers. The soldiers wore rosaries around their necks as they entered battle and prayed to the patron saint of Cuba, the Virgin Caridad del Cobre.

By his own admission, Castro never had an authentic religious faith: "I did not acquire a religious faith."[63] However, it is evident that he was in an environment that was saturated with religious beliefs.

It was not until after the breaking of diplomatic ties with the U.S. that growing economic dependence on Eastern bloc countries brought in Marxist-Leninist ideology, so it was not at first deeply ingrained. Then, following the hard-line policies of the 1960s, Fidel's regional travels in the 1970s influenced him once again to open his stance toward religion.

In 1971, Castro visited Chile under the government of Salvador Allende and met with a group called *Cristianos por el Socialismo* (Christians for Socialism). This encounter exposed Castro to the compatibility between Christianity and socialism.[64] In October 1977, the Cuban head of state traveled to Jamaica during Michael Manley's administration and met with a group of Protestant pastors.[65] Although these were brief visits, Castro was exposed to progressive Christians with a social conscience.

Meanwhile liberation theology, a post-Cuban revolutionary phenomenon, began to swell in Latin America. In July 1980 Fidel Castro traveled to Nicaragua to celebrate the first anniversary of the Sandinista Revolution, where Christians had played a key role in the overthrow of the Somoza dictatorship and the subsequent social reforms. Upsetting Castro's stereotypes, three priests, Miguel D'Escoto and Fernando and Ernesto Cardinal, held cabinet positions in the Sandinista government. These encounters played a key role in the evolution of Castro's thought toward religion.

U.S. presidential candidate Rev. Jesse Jackson's visit to Cuba also made a major impact on Fidel Castro, Cuban society, and church-state relations in general. Bishop Joel Ajo, who invited Rev. Jackson to preach from his pulpit, recalled: "He arrived at a time when relations were tense between the church and state, and after his visit there was an immediate change."[66] It was during this visit that Castro made his first appearance in a Protestant church since the triumph of the Revolution.[67] Bishop Ajo remembers:

"Rev. Jackson had just completed a lecture in the honor of Martin Luther King, Jr., at the University of *La Habana*. The next stop on Jackson's itinerary was an ecumenical worship service at the Vedado Methodist Church, where I was the pastor, about two blocks from the university. Castro accompanied Jackson to the church and as they reached the steps, Jackson invited

Castro to come inside."[68] When Castro entered the sanctuary, the already assembled congregation broke out in applause.

Rev. Jackson had the unique ability to relate equally well both to the government authorities and to the Christian community. When the Central Committee of the Communist Party said their farewells, Jackson invited all of them to hold hands and share in a moment of prayer.[69] Dr. Carneado highlighted the significance of Jackson's visit: "I almost would say that Jackson, with his presence here in Cuba and the impact of his personality, certified the initiation of the change that has taken place."[70]

Another key step in Fidel's evolution was the 1985 publication of the book *Fidel y La Religion* (*Fidel and Religion*) by Frei Betto, a Dominican priest from Brazil. Based on 23 hours of private interviews with Castro, Betto enumerated the Cuban leader's childhood experiences with religion, religious education, Marxist literature, religious leaders, liberation theology and Jesus Christ. In addition, the Cuban bestseller examined Castro's efforts to invite Pope John Paul II to Cuba, as well as areas of convergence between Christianity and revolutionary thought.

On this subject Castro states, "Throughout all these years, I have had the opportunity to express the coherency that exists between Christian thought and revolutionary thought."[71] *Fidel and Religion* was widely read in Cuba and had a transforming impact on church-state relations.

Continuing his travels, Castro visited the Base Christian Communities of Brazil in 1987. He was impressed with the social programs among the poor and was quoted in the newspaper as saying: "If we had Christians like this back in Cuba, then we would not have any problems with Christianity."[72] This was printed in the Cuban media, to which several Christians reacted by writing letters to Rev.

Raul Suarez, then president of the Cuban Ecumenical Council of Churches (CEC). Suarez, in turn, wrote to President Castro requesting a meeting.

This historic encounter between the leaders of the Cuban Ecumenical Council of Churches and President Castro took place on April 2, 1990. The meeting was videotaped and later broadcast twice on Cuban television, making a major impact on Cuban society. Although there had been an earlier meeting in 1985 between the leadership of the CEC and Castro, this one was much more significant because of its wide participation and open agenda.

The encounter began with prepared statements from the president of the CEC, Rev. Suarez, and other leaders, but it had an open agenda for any questions or comments. The turning point occurred when Rev. Joel Ajo, then president of the Methodist Church in Cuba, picked up on a phrase of the previous speaker, Rev. Otoniel Bermudez, who had said, "We have not come here to bring you any petitions or demands." Reacting against this comment Rev. Ajo said:

"We have to speak on behalf of our congregations where there are brothers and sisters who have wanted to study to become psychologists, but they have not been able to because it has been pointed out that they are Christians. They have wanted to do something, wanted to occupy an important position, for example in the Popular Power [parliament], but they haven't been able to because it has been pointed out, 'This person is Christian.' And we believe that the principal leader of our Revolution should be aware of all of this, just as Dr. Carneado is, to whom we have expressed the problems that we are confronting on several occasions. In this hour of definition where the evangelical church says that we will stay in Cuba working for the well-being of our people and to back the Revolution in all that is just, we believe the correct thing to do is to tell the Revolution where we do not agree."[73]

Castro's response was edited from the video; however, Ajo recalls that he said, "It is true that we have discriminated against Christians, and this must stop."[74] He also used his charisma and biblical knowledge to lighten the situation: "At least we haven't put you in the lion's den."[75] It is through this open and frank dialogue that the church has developed a working relationship with the state, and Fidel Castro has acquired greater appreciation for the contributions of Christians to society. But there is still much improvement to be made in religious freedom.

Church-State Relations, 1990 to the Present

This dialogue set the stage for official changes in the Communist Party policy. In October of 1991, the Communist Party held its fourth Congress to discuss the critical situation caused by the collapse of the Soviet Union. Among the many critical matters on the agenda was church-state relations. There were lengthy debates on the floor about the role of the church in a socialist society and the vote could have gone either way. Finally, three constitutional changes were approved: 1) officially changing from an atheist to a secular state; 2) permitting qualified candidates to join the Communist Party regardless of religious beliefs; and 3) adding religious freedom to the list of human rights protected by the state.

In the midst of a heated debate that could have gone either way, Eusebio Leal, historian of the City of Havana, delivered a moving speech recalling patriotic heroes, such as Frank Pais, who had fought in the war of independence and the Revolution motivated by religious convictions.[76] The Congress voted to lift legal barriers between believers and non-believers and allow for equal participation in society. Although this legislative battle was won, the decade of the 1990s would be spent fighting battles with dogmatic party officials who held key governmental posts.

Another important step occurred in December 1991 when the Cuban Ecumenical Council of Churches hosted the *Encuentro Intercontinental de Solidaridad con la Iglesia Cubana* (Intercontinental Encounter in Solidarity with the Cuban Church). The event culminated with another historic meeting with Fidel Castro. This was a closed-door encounter between Castro, Cuban ecumenical leaders, and foreign delegates representing the National Council of Churches of Christ (U.S.A.), the Canadian Council of Churches, the Latin American Council of Churches, the Caribbean Council of Churches, the European Council of Churches and one representative from the China Christian Council.

In the meeting with Castro, Rev. Joel Ajo— by then bishop of the Methodist Church in Cuba— took advantage of the public setting to confront the president directly.

A house church worships in a backyard in Jaguey Grande, Cuba

Ajo stated that although the constitution stipulated that there should be no religious gatherings off church property, for the last couple of years the churches had been conducting services in private homes, called "house churches." He recalls Castro standing up, stroking his beard and calmly responding: "You are not disobeying the constitution, you are only showing us where it needs to be amended."[77]

As a result of that encounter, the Cuban government decreed a policy by which house churches could be legally registered as places of worship.[78] Several months later the Ecumenical Council of Churches invited the leaders of the country's 54 Protestant denominations to a meeting in order to explain the procedure for registering house churches: 1) one must have the permission of the owner of the dwelling; 2) each member of the household must be in agreement; and 3) no churches of the same denomination may be located in the proximity of the house church.[79] The process of registering was very time-consuming and the government only made provision for a thousand, which was insufficient for the estimated 10,000 house churches in Cuba.[80]

Another key achievement of the encounter occurred when Joan Brown Campbell, then president of the National Council of Churches of Christ (U.S.A.), spoke on the floor and was granted permission by Castro himself for the Cuban church to be a channel for humanitarian aid from church relief organizations abroad.[81]

A further step forward between the Socialist government and the church was the granting of permission for the first Protestant missionaries from the United States to work and reside in Cuba. In the fall of 1992, the Methodist Church in Cuba negotiated permission with Dr. José Felipe Carneado of the Central Committee's Office of Religious Affairs for an official visa to receive the first long-

Phil & Diana beside Russian Car (photo: Stanley Campbell).

term missionaries of any Protestant denomination in Cuba. My wife Diana and myself are pleased to have been granted this privilege, along with our two children, Massiel and Keffren.

I had traveled to Cuba alone for three months the previous fall to learn about the Cuban church and society. Our family arrived on October 13, one day after the 500-year commemoration of Columbus's arrival in the New World. It was our hope to break with the colonial model of mission and participate in God's mission of accompaniment and support for self-determination.

In November the first caravan of Pastors for Peace arrived in Cuba in defiance of the U.S. embargo. Their arrival received much national press and Castro publicly thanked them for their heroic efforts to defy the blockade by delivering humanitarian supplies to Cuba.[82] Castro personally thanked the participants during his second appearance at a Protestant church, Ebenezer Baptist Church in Havana. Hosted by Rev. Raul Saurez and the Martin Luther King Jr. Center, the caravan brought humanitar-

Rev. Raul Saurez awaits the arrival of Pastors for Peace outside the Martin Luther King, Jr. Center in Havana.

ian supplies and then toured government hospitals and schools.

The Council of Evangelical Methodist Churches in Latin America and the Caribbean (CIEMAL) held their 5th General Assembly in Havana from March 29-April 4, 1993. This event began with the sad news of the passing of Dr. José Felipe Carneado at the age of 78. Although several Methodist leaders took time off to attend the funeral, the assembly continued as planned.

The assembly culminated with a two-and-a-half hour meeting with Fidel Castro. The Methodist leaders were able to speak with the Cuban president and educate him about Methodist history, doctrine and social concerns. Rather than coming with a specific agenda, I recall Castro being uncharacteristically quiet and inquisitive about the

Methodist Church.

The meeting met with controversy when the Cuban delegates opposed an otherwise unanimous resolution condemning the U.S. embargo. The three Cuban delegates argued to no avail that the resolution should not blame all of Cuba's hardships on the United States, but should also hold the Cuban government accountable. After publicly expressing their views, the three delegates faced persecution and eventually abandoned the country.

Following Carneado's death, the Office of Religious Affairs continued to operate under the interim leadership of Silvio Platero, longtime assistant to Dr. Carneado. Although capable and knowledgeable, neither Platero nor his successor would ever approach the respect that Dr. Carneado had acquired within the Central Committee of the Communist Party. In January 1995, the new chief of the Office of Religious Affairs was installed. Caridad Diego, a younger member of the Central Committee, was a capable woman in her early fifties, yet was more "hardline," having learned her ideology in Soviet schools rather than during the Cuban revolutionary struggle.

In the early 1990s the Cuban state was in a perilous position. They had lost their major ally and trading partner in the Soviet Union. They were facing economic shortages and a disgruntled population at home, and could ill afford to make another enemy of the growing religious sector. The Christian church, in particular, was the largest non-governmental body that enjoyed freedom of assembly, and was growing in size and authority. Moreover, Cuba was re-establishing political and economic ties with Latin American countrires, which were historically very religious. In light of this predicament, the Cuban government made several further strategic moves to warm relations with the church.

Beginning in the early 1990s, the government granted the church unprecedented liberties. After previously permitting only a trickle, the floodgates were opened for the International Bible Society to send Bibles to the Biblical Commission of the Ecumenical Council of Churches (now called the Cuban Council of Churches).[83] As a matter of fact, *Fidel and Religion* was replaced by the Bible as the best-seller in Cuban bookstores. In addition, greater leeway was granted to the churches to receive more foreign visitors and for church leaders to travel abroad.

Church Relations Abroad

As the churches strengthened their international ties, more monetary contributions increased their buying power at home, thus converting them into good customers for state-run businesses. Growing churches required electronic equipment, food and building materials, and now had the dollars to purchase them. Representatives of foreign mission boards were able to negoti-

Officials from the General Board of Global Ministries and the Methodist Church in Cuba finance a governmental housing project for hurricane victims

ate greater privileges for their Cuban partners by agreeing with the Office of Religious Affairs to invest more in social programs to meet the needs of Cuban society in the areas of health care, education and housing. The National Council of Churches (U.S.A.) sent planeloads of medicines to alleviate the shortages in Cuba. Although opening up to the church involved a calculated ideological loss for the state, there were also concrete material benefits.

In 1997 the annual conferences of Cuba and Florida rekindled the historical ties that had made them part of the same conference until Cuba's autonomy in 1968. On May 29 Bishop Cornelius L. Henderson and Rev. Rinaldo Hernández Torres, representing their respective conferences, signed the Cuba-Florida covenant calling for partnerships and cooperation. To date, this has led to visits from both sides and approximately 160 "sister church" relationships.

Pope John Paul II's visit to Cuba in 1998 also had a tremendous effect on church-state relations, even for the Protestant church. Although Fidel Castro issued the invitation to the pontiff as a guest of the state, his visit very clearly had religious, social and political implications for the entire nation. Saying mass in Santiago, Santa Clara and Havana, the Pope called upon the state to allow greater church participation in society. He also urged Catholics to participate in a national dialogue. Even though some conservative evangelicals were concerned that the Pope's visit might strengthen the Roman Catholic Church, one cannot deny the universality of his liberating message for the well-being of all Cubans.

The Pope's visit brought a lot of international attention and scrutiny to Cuba, which helped generate more religious freedom for a short time. Most Cubans, however, felt that there were no long-lasting benefits of the

Pope's visit.

Fidel Castro continues to govern Cuba and make symbolic gestures to the church without allowing complete religious freedom. For example, in 1998 the government allowed Christmas trees— long a taboo symbol of the West's superstition— to be placed in government stores and public places. Whether motivated by goodwill or consumerism, this is one example of how Cuba's policy toward the church makes conciliatory gestures. More recently, on April 25, 2004, Castro attended his first mass— outside of the Pope's visit— when he was present at the consecration of a newly constructed Byzantine Catholic Church in Havana.

In summary, the relationship between the church and the state in Cuba is the result of a long process, unique to Cuban history. In addition, there have been foreign influences from Spanish priests, North American missionaries, mission boards, and Soviet Marxism-Leninism. In spite of all the changes in Cuban history, the people have generally remained religious. Under the Castro regime, church-state relations became tense following the declaration of the socialist character of the Revolution. Over the years both sides have dialogued to understand each other better, with the active participation of Dr. Jose Felipe Carneado, a key figure in the process. The encounters of President Fidel Castro with progressive Christians and the visits of Father Frei Betto and Rev. Jesse Jackson to Cuba also made important contributions. After the collapse of the Soviet Union, the Cuban government has opened up toward religion. However, following the death of Dr. Carneado, some of these privileges have been rescinded.

In the mid to late 1990s the church and the state continue to have cordial relations, although they are characterized by an unequal relationship of power.

FOOTNOTES

38   Frei Betto, *Fidel and Religion* (interviews with Fidel Castro),
Oficina de Publicaciones del Consejo de Estado, 1985, p.277.

39   Gomez Treto, Raoul, *La Iglesia Catolica durante la Construccion del
Socialism en Cuba*, CEHILA, 1994, p.44.

40   Ibid.

41   Ibid, p.48.

42   Betto, p.144.

43   Ibid, p.277.

44   Gomez Treto, p.48.

45   Israel Batista, "*El Protestantismo Cubano en un Proyecto Historico*,"
La Herencia Misionera en Cuba, San Jose: DEI, 1996, p.65.

46   Carlos Camps Cruell, "*La Herencia Misionera en Cuba:
Implicaciones en los Social*," *La Herencia Misionera en Cuba*, Rafael
Cepeda (ed.). San Jose: DEI, 1996, pp.123-130. My translation.

47   Carlos Perez, *Un Resumen de los Setenta Anos de Labor de la Iglesia
Metodista en Cuba, 1898-1968*, (self-published) Miami, 1983, p.46.

48   Interview with Bishop Armando Rodriguez, Sr. in Des
Plaines, Illinois, January 20, 1998.

49   Interview with Bishop Joel Ajo in Racine, Wisconsin, April 8,
1998.

50   Interview with Bishop Armando Rodriguez, Sr. in Des
Plaines, Illinois, January 20, 1998.

51   "*Con Dios y Con la Patria*," video of encounter between Consejo
Ecumenico de Cuba and Fidel Castro, April 2, 1990.

52   Shawn T. Malone, "Conflict, Coexistence, and Cooperation:
Church-State Relations in Cuba," Georgetown University, Center
for Latin American Studies, August 1996, p.3.

53   "God's Time for Cuba," Window on the World, *Bibles
International*, Vol.7, No.1.

54   Interview with Bishop Joel Ajo in Racine, Wisconsin, April 8,
1998.

55   Quoted in Alvarez, p.23. My translation.

56   Quoted in Carmelo Alvarez, *Cuba: Testimonio Cristiano, Vivencia
Revolucionaria*, San Jose: DEI, 1990, p.23.

57   Ibid, p.34.

58   Betto, p.109.

59   Ibid, p.115, p.126.

60   Ibid, pp.140-1.

61   Ibid, p.144.

62   Ibid, p.163.

63   Ibid, p.322. My translation.

64   Ibid, p.273.

65   Ibid, p.274.

66   Interview with Bishop Joel Ajo in Racine, Wisconsin, April 8, 1998.

67   Malone, p.3.

68   Interview with Bishop Joel Ajo in Racine, Wisconsin, April 8, 1998.

69   Ibid.

70   Carmelo Alvarez, p.44.

71   Ibid, p.322. My translation.

72   *"Con Dios y Con la Patria."*

73   Ibid. My translation.

74   Interview with Bishop Joel Ajo in Racine, Wisconsin, April 8, 1998.

75   Ibid.

76   Ibid.

77   Personal notes.

78   John W. Kennedy, "Cuba's Next Revolution," *Christianity Today*, January 12, 1998, p.22.

79   Philip Wingeier-Rayo and Paul Chilcote, "The Wesleyan Revival and Methodism in Cuba," *Quarterly Review*, Vol.17, No.3, Fall 1997, p.215.

80   Malone, p.8.

81   Ibid.

82   Personal notes.

83   Malone, p.8.

Chapter IV

Revival Within the Methodist Church in Cuba

This chapter will analyze the origins, theology and worship style— with particular emphasis on charismatic manifestations— of the revival movement within the Cuban Methodist Church. The two rises of the movement will be outlined, and the growth and spread of the revival will be described.

The Arrival of Methodism in Cuba

The Spanish conquest of Cuba brought Catholicism to the indigenous population, and later it was imposed upon the African slaves. Overall, the Roman Catholic Church was well entrenched, but only among the elite and *criollos* (creoles), while the grassroots religion was Afro-Cuban Santeria. Prior to U.S. occupation in the aftermath of the Spanish-American War in 1898, Protestantism was not legal, although there was some relaxation in the late 1800s.

The history of Methodism in Cuba can be traced back to 1883 when the Florida Annual Conference sent Enrique B. Someillan and Aurelio Silvera as missionaries.[84] They started a congregation which worshiped at the Saratoga Hotel on Galiano Street in Havana.[85] Someillan had come to the United States with his brother at the age of 13 because his father was deported from Cuba for opposing the

Spanish Crown in 1869.[86] Someillan was moved by the final words of Rev. Joseph E.A. Vanduzer, who had established the groundwork with the Cuban mission in Key West in 1874. Vanduzer died of yellow fever a year later, and stated on his deathbed, "Don't give up the Cuban mission."[87]

By 1888 Someillan had returned to Florida, but Silvera remained with a congregation of 194 in Havana and wrote back to the Florida Annual Conference requesting recognition.[88] That same year J.J. Ranson, who had worked in Brazil, answered a request for missionaries and served the Cuban mission from 1888-91.[89] Isidero Barredo, a product of the early Cuban mission, became a licensed preacher and led the congregation from 1893 through the War of Independence in 1895. At that time the congregation was dispersed, but Barredo was noted for his efforts in support of Cuba's independence.[90]

On November 23, 1898, immediately following the War of Independence (Spanish-American War), Bishop Warren A. Candler of Florida and his wife departed for Cuba to round up the disbanded congregation and offer more missionary support. H.W. Baker accompanied the bishop on that journey and stayed on to continue the work. Requesting a second opinion from someone with more experience in the Latin American mission field, Bishop Candler and Dr. Lambeth, head of the Board of Missions of the Methodist Episcopal Church, South, invited David W. Carter to visit Cuba in February 1899 from his post in Mexico.[91] He returned very enthusiastic about the prospect for Protestant mission work and recorded in his report:

"The revolt from Romanism is almost universal. Hatred of it has led to religious indifference and skepticism . . . I asked an intelligent physician in Cienfuegos why there seemed to be so little religious life among the

Cubans. His reply was pathetic. Said he: 'It is not our fault. The priests are so corrupt and mercenary and have made such merchandise of religion that we have lost all respect for them and their church.'"[92]

On January 1, 1899, the Spanish flag was lowered and the American flag was raised, beginning four years of U.S. military occupation. Shortly after, the Florida Annual Conference appointed several pastors, including Someillan, Barredo and Baker, to mission sites in Havana, Matanzas, Cardenas, Cienfuegos, Santiago and Manzanillo.[93]

Sterling Augustus Neblett, a missionary who entered Cuba in 1902 and later wrote *Methodism's First Fifty Years in Cuba*, made this comparison between the U.S. military occupation of Cuba and the missionary initiative: "The entrance of God's messengers, who were few in number and who came to bring peace and safety to the Cuban people,

Old Methodist School before the Revolution
(photo: Santa Fe Methodist Church archives).

was militant but not military."[94] He also referred to the expansion of Methodism following the Spanish-American War as "occupation."[95]

The expansion of Methodism was very well planned in Cuba. By the end of the first decade of the new initiative, there were 33 preachers, 15 of them Cuban, 43 Sunday schools, 14 Methodist youth groups, more than 600 students registered in schools, and some 3,000 members and candidates, with 32 churches and chapels.[96]

Originally this mission work was done under the auspices of the Florida Annual Conference. Beginning in 1919, however, a Cuban missionary conference was organized. In 1923 a Cuban Annual Conference (not missionary) was formed with the bishop of Florida presiding. The idea of autonomy was already present, although it would not become a reality until many years later.[97] The Methodist Church was known for offering many social services to the Cuban people. Schools, medical dispensaries and literacy campaigns were prevalent. The conference continued to expand through the building of new churches and parsonages.

Although the different denominations working in Cuba, had always collaborated, the Cuban Council of Evangelical Churches was not founded until May 20, 1940. One of its first fruits was an ecumenical seminary, the Seminario Evangelico de Teologia in Matanzas, which opened its doors on October 1, 1946, housed in school buildings and grounds donated by the Women's Society of Christian Service of the Methodist Church.[98]

By 1959 there were 51 Cuban pastors and 54 U.S. missionaries serving 150 preaching places, 22 schools, six dispensaries, and several rural missions.[99] The Methodist Church had 9,209 members.[100] This was a church highly dependent on North American Methodism, and wholly unprepared for the changes that were to come.

Methodism Under the Revolution

In the days following dictator Fulgencio Batista's departure from Cuba on January 1, 1959, Fidel Castro's *Movimiento 26 de Julio*— named after that initial failed attack on the Santiago armory on July 26, 1953—caravaned from Cuba's eastern mountains to claim power in Havana. The grassroots movement had swelled until its victory on New Year's day, at which time the overwhelming majority of the population was supportive of the Revolution and its early reforms in health care, literacy and land redistribution. The problems with the church began when Castro declared the Revolution to be socialist on the eve of the Bay of Pigs invasion on April 17, 1961.

The United States had broken off diplomatic ties with the island three months earlier following Cuba's nationalization of American-owned oil refineries. With relations tense between the United States and Cuba, anti-American sentiments were growing. The Cuban Methodists were beginning to be stigmatized for being pro-North American, and therefore asked the U.S. missionaries to return home for the well-being of the Methodist Church and its pastors.[101] Cubans also feared for the safety of the missionaries and their families. The Methodist Board of Missions recalled all mission personnel, and many Cuban pastors were soon to follow. Many people thought the churches would be closed. Some missionaries issued invitations to their favorite Cuban pastors to immigrate to the United States. Eventually all but eight of the 51 Cuban pastors would flee the country.[102]

Lacking pastors and confronting the growing anti-religious sentiment, the Methodist Church faced an extremely challenging period in the early 1960s. Not only was the church weakened through emigration; in addition many lay people left the church for greater opportunity or out of loyalty to the Revolution.[103] Nevertheless there was a remnant that remained faithful. The District Superintendent of Cuba's Oriente region, Rev. Armando Rodríguez, had trained a group of young men and women to be lay missioners. As the churches were left without pastors, he asked this group to replace those who had left. Lacking theological education and experience, these young lay people heroically served those churches, often living on the premises, protecting church property from vandalism and confiscation.[104]

One of the most valiant efforts to save church property was made by Dr. Orlando Rovira, who literally placed his life in the line of fire. A member of the University Methodist Church, Dr. Rovira confronted government agents and slept in the recently built University Center to protect it from nationalization. He is now deceased, but his widow, Ysel Pérez, is still a member of the church, now called Vedado Methodist Church, and lives to tell the tale. Although this is one of many heroic stories, there are several cases of vacant properties being confiscated.

In the early 1960s the Cuban church, cut off from regular communication and transfer of funds from the North American church, was facing a financial crisis. They had been receiving nearly 70 percent of their financial resources from the United States, and had also lost the income generated from Methodist schools after their nationalization. In July 1963, Rev. Angel Fuster, president of the Cuban Annual Conference, received the news from the head of the Latin America desk of the Methodist Mission Board, Dr. Eugene Stockwell, that financial support could no longer be disbursed due to the U.S. embargo of Cuba.

In response the Cuban cabinet proposed three options: lay off half the pastors (those who enjoyed less seniority), ask the revolutionary government for compensation for the nationalized properties, or request the local churches to send apportionments to the national church. The Cuban leadership valiantly chose the third option, and within two months the national church was solvent.[105] The early enthusiasm and nationalistic spirit also influenced the church leaders' desire to be independent.[106] Financial self-sufficiency prepared the groundwork for autonomy.

In 1967 the Cuban Annual Conference voted to become autonomous from North American Methodism. Tragically, Rev. Angel Fuster, the logical candidate to become the church's first Cuban bishop, was killed on January 5, 1967, in an automobile accident. Consequently, on February 11, 1968, Armando Rodríguez Sr. was consecrated as the first Cuban bishop of the Methodist Church in Cuba, and a new period was born. Pending approval of the uniting conference in Dallas, Texas, the new Methodist Church in Cuba was to become an autonomous affiliated church and retains this relationship with The United Methodist Church today.

In spite of losing most of its clergy, and having its membership dip to 5,000,[107] the Cuban Methodist Church had survived the hardest times. The military work camps (*Unidades Militares de Ayuda a la Produccion*) were closed, and the state had begun to develop a policy of tolerance and respect toward religion. Inside the Methodist Church there were also some signs of renewal.

The First Rise of the Revival[108]

The exodus of missionaries and pastors also meant the loss of the best theologically trained leaders. Although new pastors began to enter the ministry, the urgency was so great that there was no time to send them for seminary training. Due to the lack of clergy, the Methodist Church began to accept pastors from other denominations.[109] This permitted doctrines and forms of worship alien to Methodism to enter the conference.

As early as 1968 there were three pastors from Pentecostal origins, Ariel González, Walby Leja and Luis Pérez Leal, who pastored churches in La Ceiba, Camaguey and in the rural area of Frei Benito, respectively.[110] These three pastors formed the nucleus of a movement with a different form of worship, which included singing choruses and clapping hands. They practiced laying on hands and being "slain in the Spirit" (falling). They also introduced the theology of the Second Blessing and opposed infant baptism. There were even public confrontations with the conference leadership, as Ariel González and his followers would interrupt Methodist worship services. Once when Bishop Rodríguez attempted to re-inaugurate the Methodist Church in Cacocun in 1973, the police were called in to break up a disturbance.[111]

This Pentecostal group continued to grow until June 1973, when 12 pastors presented a demand to the annual conference that they would resign unless there were changes in *The Book of Discipline*. This constituted a direct challenge to the authority of Bishop Rodríguez.[112] However several lay people, including Orlando Rovira and Rinaldo Hernández Blanco, volunteered to replace those pastors if they were to resign, thus undercutting the strength of the protest.[113] The movement failed to find a fertile reception in the conference, and the rebel pastors resigned their positions. Some tried to re-enter the conference later and were accepted, although the three principal leaders never returned. Ariel González created a schism and occupies the Methodist parsonage in Omaja to this day.[114]

This movement did, however, have a lasting effect on the Methodist Church. Shortly after the exodus of the rebels, Methodist pastors Emilio González (no relation to

Ariel González) and Rafael Gonzalo Calzado began the practice of singing choruses. Although these pastors knew of the previous movement, they claimed to have a different origin. Rev. Emilio González explains why the earlier movement failed:

"The people who directed the movement were not ready for a revival because they brought in aspects that did not belong to the revival. In the movement one has to be very careful not to mistreat anyone but to love everyone. The problem is when we start to criticize someone because that person does not think like you, then you have a big spiritual confrontation and the lines [of communication] with the Lord are closed, in the sense that you are closing doors that you do not know. You do not know what plans God might have for those people."[115] In retrospect, González felt that the early charismatic movement lacked the love and openness that should characterize a true revival.

As one of the early proponents of spiritual revival, González experienced unusual physical manifestations of the Holy Spirit on his own. He relates an early experience with a supernatural smell of perfume: "The perfume smell manifested itself in worship services, but the first time, I was alone. In the house we do not have perfume. In addition to the fact that one could not find perfume at that time, my wife did not use perfume because she is asthmatic. But that experience was so real that there was no doubt in my mind that it was perfume. I could not understand it; it was supernatural."[116]

As these experiences continued, González shared them with a group of pastors as they met to pray following extension courses, when anyone was welcome to stay and ask questions. Singing choruses, speaking in tongues, and falling ("slain in the Spirit") were practiced in this group.[117] Though these practices became more and more common within the group, they were not immediately prominent in most Methodist churches. González describes the first part of the movement as being very quiet: "It was a revival without any noise. It was the quietest in the world."[118]

Charismatic manifestations became more and more common at Methodist Youth League assemblies. González was assigned to be the national advisor to the Methodist Youth League between 1987 and 1989, during which time manifestations of the Holy Spirit, especially being "slain in the Spirit," were prominent at the assemblies.[119]

These manifestations were not practiced without objection from many Cuban Methodists. There was a large sector of the annual conference that had strongly opposed the first group of twelve pastors, and continued to oppose any similar phenomenon.[120] Eventually the Methodist clergy would become polarized over this issue. One of the controversial theological topics was being "slain in the Spirit." Some argued in favor, others against. González explains:

"Falling occurred back then although it was not that frequent because it was not considered to be a blessing. It was considered to be like a faint in the presence of the Spirit that would not occur if the person were spiritually prepared. Some people fell, but the object was to try not to fall. Nobody touched them. There was a spiritual confrontation when the Lord came and if one were not prepared, one would faint."[121]

During a pastors' retreat in 1984 at the Vedado Methodist Church, a group of pastors were discussing the issue of being "slain in the Spirit." One confident young pastor offered to lay hands on all the opposing clergy, promising a "slaying." González suggested another means of resolving the impasse; the pastors stood in a circle and each placed his hand on the person next to him and prayed. If it was the will of God for someone to fall, the Spirit would be free to touch people on an individual basis. After praying for a while, none of them had fallen.

Then González spoke in tongues and interpreted the following message: "While four fall, there are six that remain standing. Those who fall do so because they do not resist my presence. I want a strong church that does not fall."[122] In spite of this message and discussion, the difference of opinion about these manifestations continued.

The early 1980s also brought a greater interest in the 18th-century Methodist revival. It was pointed out that there were unusual manifestations and falling or fainting during Wesley's time. González began placing more emphasis on the Wesleyan roots of the emerging revival within the Methodist Church.[123] This effort was greatly hampered by the scarcity of accurate Wesleyan literature in Cuba at that time. It was not until 1998 that Justo González finished translating the first six volumes of Wesley's works into Spanish and distribution began on the island.[124]

The Second Rise of the Revival

In the late 1980s the growing sector of the Methodist Church which believed in these manifestations began to produce young candidates for the ministry. One of those was 16 year-old Ernesto Betancourt of Pinar del Rio. Betancourt was assigned by the senior pastor, Rev. Ricardo Pereira, to pastor a small congregation in Entronque de Herradura.

Now a District Superintendent, Rev. Betancourt recalls his prayer during his first pastoral charge: "Lord, I want you to clarify to me what is my ministry. I am not satisfied with a church of 20 people when there are many who walk past the church and need you. Lord, if this church continues like this I will withdraw from the pastorate because I will think that you have not called me."[125] He received the answer to his prayer with the arrival of an evangelist in 1989. He recalls:

"One afternoon a blond peasant named Ramiro Expósito arrived from eastern Cuba and said to Ricardo [Pereira] that he was an evangelist from a Pentecostal church. And he said, 'I am here, pastor, because God sent me and although you do not know me, I come from God. He told me to come to the Methodist Church in Pinar del Rio because He is going to do great things here; and I want to preach tonight. You will see with your own eyes what God will do.' Ricardo accepted because it seemed that he received confirmation from God, and that night the Lord started to do great things in the church, like touch lives, fill cavities, and raise the paralyzed during a one-week campaign."[126]

Shortly after this, Expósito was offered an appointment pastoring a rural mission of the Pinar del Rio church called Fusilazo. Bishop Rodríguez recognized his work and eventually he was received as a pastor in the annual conference.[127] In 1989 Expósito led an evangelistic crusade in Entronque de Herradura. Many manifestations of the Holy Spirit, such as healings, "slayings" and speaking in tongues, were reported. Following the crusade, under the leadership of Pastor Ernesto Betancourt, the congregation grew to be more than a hundred people. Manifestations of the Holy Spirit were prevalent. Bishop Rodríguez went to visit one day unannounced to confirm the reports.[128]

In 1989 this charismatic style began to grow across the Methodist Church in Cuba. Another evangelistic crusade was organized in the Central District. Betancourt recalls: "The revival in Entroque de Herradura had been going on for four months when the national Evangelism

Commission [of the Methodist Church] sent me on a campaign to Caonao, near the city of Cienfuegos. When I began to pray for this, the Lord told me, 'Don't go alone because this will be bigger than what you have seen these days here. Take Ricardo, my servant.'

"We went quickly to Cienfuegos and after a long trip, when we finally arrived in Caonao at eight o'clock in the evening, we found the church overflowing. We immediately began to preach and the Lord started to heal. This started to promote itself in such a way that we preached the gospel to nearly all of Cienfuegos. The services were in the open air and this is why it was bigger than Pinar del Rio. Even the authorities called us to find out who we were, because many people talked to them about us. But we did not have any problems with them; they even took care of the [public] order."[129]

The group continued their crusade across Cuba, having many manifestations of the Holy Spirit in places like Manicaragua and San Juan de los Yeras, until it was finally stopped by the authorities in Santa Clara.[130]

Also in 1989, the annual conference appointed Hildelisa Amores as pastor of the Marianao Methodist Church in Havana, but she was awaiting a visa to the United States and left mid-year, creating a vacancy. A seminary student from Angola, Moises Domingo Fernándes (now bishop of the Methodist Church in Angola), was asked to attend to the church, but this was problematic. He did not speak fluent Spanish, and could only be present on the weekends due to his full-time class schedule at the seminary in Matanzas. Therefore an active lay couple, Jesus Expósito (no relation to Ramiro Expósito) and his wife Cristy, took on a leadership role.

Expósito, an evangelist and graduate of a non-Methodist seminary, was not an ordinary layperson. Earlier he had received a vision from the Lord calling him to pastor the church, although he was denied an appointment by the cabinet.[131] The Marianao Church was an example of how a church became susceptible to outside influences due to the shortage of Methodist pastors. In addition, the discrimination faced by Christians on a daily basis took its toll, and any leader who sparked growth and enthusiasm seemed attractive. Guido Benazet, who later became a member of the Marianao Church, explains this phenomenon:

"For some reason, God changed 'his strategy' from a revival through healings of the multitudes and well-known leaders to a revival through local churches and almost unknown pastors, where healings occurred sporadically. These were spiritually weak churches with few young people. Then, one day a pastor arrives full of the Holy Spirit, willing to teach the congregation about the baptism of Jesus, the gifts of the Spirit and a life of prayer and fasting."[132]

A revival began in Marianao and many young people, particularly Juan Carlos González, became active proponents of the charismatic renewal. The movement grew rapidly during the first year, with much emphasis on prayer and fasting. The following year, 1990, the annual conference appointed an ordained elder named Rev. Rinaldo Hernández Torres to be pastor. But the movement had so much power that it could not be controlled (see Chapter 1). My first visit to this congregation was a year later in 1991 and I witnessed an obvious Pentecostal influence on the congregation.[133]

The events of 1989— the impact of Ramiro Expósito, Ernesto Betancourt and Jesus Expósito, the crusades in Pinar del Rio and the Central District— are considered by Rev. Emilio González to be the second stage of the revival. He distinguishes between the first stage, contained within the church and quieter in nature, and the second stage when it transcended the church and reached out to the masses:

"This was a second part that had to do with the masses. It had to do with all the churches. It was a continuation; first came one part and then the other. In this second part it was not only the Methodist Church, rather it extended to all the churches. It was something that spilled out beyond a certain denomination."[134]

This second rise of the Cuban revival both influenced and was influenced by other denominations inside and outside of Cuba.

Improved church-state relations in the early 1990s allowed for more visitors from abroad, which naturally contributed to greater outside influence. The meeting between Fidel Castro and leaders of the Ecumenical Council of Churches on April 2, 1990, marked the beginning of the Cuban government's relaxation of restrictions on the church.[135] This permitted the arrival of many North American "missionaries" traveling to Cuba through the Dominican Republic and entering the country on tourist visas. Bishop Ajo recalls a religious "offensive" toward the interior of Cuba in the early nineties.[136]

Ricardo Luna and the Tamez brothers were representatives of Open Doors, a North American Christian organization with known ties to the religious right, which contributed Spanish Bibles and money to Cuban churches.[137] *Hermanos Castro* was another organization led by two Puerto Rican pastors who traveled to Cuba with donations.[138] Well-known evangelists visited Cuba, such as Freddy, *"El Brujo,"* who visited Pinar del Rio under the auspices of the Methodist Church in Cuba.[139] In November 1993, a group of young people from the United States visited Cuba representing the organization Teen Mania.[140]

Perhaps the most telling example of the government's opening was the arrival of John Stemkoski's Celebrant

Singers. This evangelistic ministry had been denied entry on previous occasions, but when Bishop Ajo invited the group, Carneado trusted the Methodist Church enough to not only grant the visas, but also allow the first "open air" Christian concert, held in Punta Brava on November 22, 1993– right in front of our parsonage!

Since the sanctuary in our local church was small and we expected a large crowd, we petitioned the authorities to allow us to have the concert outside. Using our neighbor's porch as a stage, we set up the pews in the street and the police blocked off traffic. The attendance was even better than expected as people stood in the street to see the live spectacle.

Audio and video cassettes from abroad with Christian messages played a key role in the second rise of the revival. Rev. Betancourt expounds on the importance of this tool for expanding the influence of the movement:

"Christian people could begin to acquire tape recorders for the first time and, almost simultaneously, some Christian visitors, foreigners, brought cassettes which they gave away to the churches before leaving. The cassettes by a certain evangelist completely unknown in our country were passed around hand to hand and were copied from tape recorder to tape recorder, leaving a truckload of blessings wherever they went and notably influencing several young people. The evangelist's name: Yiye Avila."[141]

Reproductions of sermons from Yiye Avila, a famous Puerto Rican evangelist, and other tapes were also made available through the 14 distribution centers of the Methodist Church Audio-Visual Center (M.A.V.I.M.C.).[142] These were Christian tapes with musical or preached messages from a variety of denominations abroad. It is estimated that these tapes impacted the lives of nearly a million Cubans.[143]

The church and parsonage in Punta Brava where we lived.

This extensive contact with outside influences encouraged non-Wesleyan doctrine and practices. Great emphasis was placed on the gifts of the Holy Spirit, particularly speaking in tongues. In 1993 we were worshiping in our home church in Punta Brava, Cuba, when a Pentecostal preacher from England was invited to give the message. At the end of the sermon he invited the congregation to come to the altar and encouraged us to speak in tongues. During a brief pause, I went to the pulpit and whispered in his ear that he was welcome to preach the gospel, but not to impose his doctrine.

This was only one personal example of a foreign influence that was widespread. The government wanted to give the impression of freedom of religion and the church wanted foreigners to bring much-needed financial support. Therefore visitors flooded the religious arena with a plethora of doctrines, and sometimes a political message. Cubans appropriated these messages and put them into practice.

Conflict and Controversy

The government was afraid of this rapid church growth, particularly the influx of a more conservative evangelical theology. An extraordinary evangelistic campaign in the Methodist Church in Manzanillo, November 15-20, 1992, caused tension between the church and the state. Witnesses told of many supernatural healings. Each night the crowds grew until there were thousands of people in and outside of the church, even blocking the street. The police became concerned about the number of people attending the event and intervened. The principal evangelist, Juan Carlos González of the Marianao Methodist Church, was arrested and accused of disrupting the public order, but was released shortly after. The extended cabinet of the Methodist Church responded with a *"Pastoral para tiempos de crisis"* (Pastoral letter for times of crisis), which said, in part:

"Since the first night of the campaign, God began to make marvelous signs amongst those attending the worship services. Many were converted, the sick were healed, the paralyzed rose out of their wheelchairs and glorified God. The news of these signs traveled quickly amongst the population, and attendance at the worship services grew each night. On the 19th more than 700 people participated, of whom about 100 made a profession of faith and many gave testimonies about being healed in the name of Jesus. On the night of Friday the 20th, after having proclaimed the Word and issuing an invitation, about 200 people accepted the Lord. A crowd estimated between 1,500 and 2,000 people were congregated inside and outside of the church. Then people in civilian clothes took possession of the church entrance, while others went toward the altar trying to reach the preacher. One of them shouted, 'We want that pastor dead or alive.'"[144]

Although Bishop Ajo went to Manzanillo to speak

with state authorities, no satisfactory explanation was given as to why the event was disrupted.

The growth of these manifestations of the Holy Spirit in the Methodist Church was so confusing and controversial that the Methodist Commission of Theology was given the task of writing a statement about the church's doctrine of the Holy Spirit. A key issue was whether the gift of speaking in tongues was the *only* sign of receiving the seal of the Holy Spirit. The commission concluded its report, approved by the 1993 Annual Conference, by stating: "There is no biblical text that shows that one who does not speak in tongues is not full of the Holy Spirit, or has not been baptized by the Holy Spirit." The report went on to assert that speaking in tongues is biblical and is not "the exclusive right of the Pentecostal groups, but rather the common heritage of all Christians."[145] The report of this commission was sufficiently broad to allow all sectors of the church to reach their own conclusions; however, it did provide a subtle confirmation of the doctrine of the baptism of Jesus with the Holy Spirit:

"The baptism of Jesus with the Holy Spirit is the baptism which capacitates the Christian to exercise gifts and ministry with power in the church. This baptism, called by Wesley the 'second blessing,' is the experience which initiates us in a life full of the Holy Spirit and permits us to have repeated experiences filling us with the Spirit. Thus, we call the initial experience of power 'Baptism of Jesus with the Holy Spirit,' because we are filled with the Spirit. The successive experiences capacitate us for special tasks and ministries in the Church."[146]

Another phenomenon that was more frequently observed during the second rise of the revival was the *post-culto* worship services. This manifestation involves a sector of the congregation that spontaneously remains after the service for a vigil. This is often referred to in Pentecostal doctrine as "latter rain." The formal service concludes, but some members of the congregation stay to "seek the gifts of the Holy Spirit." While some may feel like the worship service did not meet all their spiritual needs and have a sincere desire to remain, others stay because of peer pressure and competition for the gifts of the Spirit. If one had not experienced a baptism of the Holy Spirit, then one was somehow less holy than the other Christians.[147] This phenomenon was particularly prominent at the Methodist Youth League assemblies.

The charismatic sector of the Methodist Church grew in numbers and in power until it acquired enough strength to compete for key church offices. In addition to the audio-visual materials and visitors, the movement also received regular financial contributions from abroad.[148]

Joel Ajo observed the spread of the movement, but tried to be bishop of the whole church. Of course, he agreed with church growth, but was suspicious of the extreme tendencies of the charismatic renewal. He also was supportive of the current government, while leaders of the movement tended to be reactionary. In November 1993 Bishop Ajo was quoted in the state-sponsored newspaper *El Granma* as supporting the efforts of Pastors for Peace.

This quote was perceived as pro-government, and Methodist members across the country were upset over what was perceived to be a public statement on behalf of the Methodist Church. Immediately members of the cabinet started a campaign to depose the bishop. The grounds for the opposition were both theological and political, but church law does not allow a bishop to be deposed on ideological grounds. Searching through *The Book of Discipline*, the opposition found a charge of "undesirable" and called for a vote at an extraordinary General

Conference, with a two-thirds majority required to depose the bishop.

The moment was very tense, since the opposition movement threatened to separate from the Methodist Church if they were not victorious in their efforts. However the same delegates who had elected the bishop three years earlier were still members of General Conference and the motion did not pass, ending in a 23-23 vote with one abstention, thus allowing Bishop Ajo to finish the remaining year of his electoral term.[149]

The special session of General Conference showed a solid group of clergy and laity that not only supported Bishop Ajo, but also were not ready for such a rapid transition to a charismatic church. This sector tended to be older and more progressive. They had decided to stay in Cuba throughout three and a half decades and had sacrificed to maintain the church under a socialist government. They had learned their style of worship from the missionaries and the charismatic renewal felt like a betrayal of their Methodist roots. This sector had earned the right to be in leadership positions and was not going to easily give up.

On the other hand, leaders of the charismatic sector were not satisfied with the vote and continued to threaten schism. Some names for a new church had already been proposed, for example *"Iglesia Metodista Carismática Apolitica."* Immediately after the close of General Conference, leaders of the disgruntled sector met in the parsonage of the Marianao Methodist Church to discuss strategy. Rev. Emilio González recalls, "I was there and can tell you that the Methodist Church would have divided. If it had not been for my voice, I can tell you that the church would have divided."[147] The leaders agreed to stay within the Methodist Church for the final year of Bishop Ajo's episcopacy, although they discontinued their apportionments to the national church.

With the regular session of the VII General Conference scheduled for March 1995, irregular events began to occur. Pastors and lay delegates were visited by strangers and called into meetings by the state security and were told that Bishop Ajo was their candidate.[151]

Then, three days before the regular session of the Seventh General Conference was to begin in March of 1995, Rev. Ricardo Pereira, leader of the charismatic sector and a leading candidate for the episcopacy, was arrested by civil authorities in Pinar del Rio on grounds that he had altered his electric bill. Rev. Pereira had been the first runner-up in the elections for bishop at the VI General Conference in 1991.

Certainly the timing of the arrest was suspicious, leading observers to believe that the government did not want Pereira to be elected. His arrest had the opposite effect, however, as delegates became sympathetic to his plight. He was released after one night in jail, but remained under house arrest.[152] After some talk of postponing General Conference, it began on schedule without Pereira. In the afternoon of the second day of conference he was permitted to leave his house and was received at conference with a standing ovation.

Although Rev. Pereira was not one of the principal vote-getters at this General Conference, his arrest had raised his popularity and threw the balance of support toward the charismatic sector of the church. In his stead Rev. Pereira supported Rev. Gustavo Cruz, his first cousin, who came to within one vote of being elected bishop. However after several ballots, continuing well past midnight, the assembly was exhausted and proposed a compromise to the impasse: interim co-presidents to direct the church for one year until another session of general conference could be called. Thus, Rev. Gustavo Cruz, the

Consecration service of Bishop Gustavo Cruz (robed).
Rev. Ricardo Pereira, now bishop, is at far right.

leading candidate, and Rev. Roy Rodríguez, vice-president of the cabinet, assumed team leadership for one year.[153]

Several months later the charges against Pereira were taken to court. He was convicted of a misdemeanor and fined 180 pesos.

The following March (1996), a special session of General Conference was called to elect a bishop. Again strange events began to occur. For example, I and several other church leaders received an anonymous letter on church letterhead that criticized the leadership of Gustavo Cruz and Roy Rodríguez and encouraged delegates to re-elect Bishop Ajo. But by then the charismatic sector had consolidated its bases and Rev. Cruz had gained necessary leadership experience. The Methodist Church in Cuba had grown so rapidly that it was now averaging 40,000 in attendance nationwide,[154] and the majority of these new converts were charismatic. After only three ballots on March 5, 1996, Rev. Gustavo Cruz was elected in a landslide victory over Rev. Roy Rodríguez, thus completing the rise to power of the charismatic sector of the church.

Sadly, almost two years into his episcopacy Bishop Cruz suffered cerebral hemorrhaging and was hospitalized. After rehabilitation at Methodist Hospital in Houston he was able to return to Cuba— although with very visible disabilities. Naming his cousin, Ricardo Pereira, as vice-president of the cabinet, he invited him to take over many administrative responsibilities.

Claiming that the four-year episcopal term should have begun in 1995 at the regular VII General Conference, Ricardo Pereira called for elections at the 1999 VIII General Conference. So, after only three years as bishop, Gustavo Cruz completed his term and assumed the title of Bishop Emeritus. In the meantime, Pereira had solidified his support base and administrative control. He produced a sweeping victory and was consecrated bishop in March of 1999. Re-elected at the IX General Conference in 2003, Bishop Pereira remains the undisputed leader of the charismatic renewal and Cuban Methodism.

Nevertheless, the longtime Methodist laity and clergy remain faithful to the church. At times they feel out of place, but they remain in the shadows, often adding wisdom and maturity to the brash young charismatic movement. Most clergy from the "old guard" have retired and continue to attend annual conference and other national events, yet their input is rarely sought. Others have tried to immigrate to the United States to begin a new career in Hispanic ministries.

In summary, the events described in this chapter mark a dramatic transition from a more traditional Methodist worship style to a charismatic expression of the faith. The charismatic revival has indeed produced prolific growth in local churches that have assumed this worship style. Membership in the Methodist Church has grown from 5,000 in 1990 to 16,000 in 2001. Actual attendance at Methodist places of worship rose from 10,000 to 45,000 during the same time period.[155] Some local churches are more charismatic than others, but all churches are growing.

This has been a painful process of metamorphosis in which a charismatic theology and worship style spread throughout the church, while traditional pastors were gradually isolated during a power struggle for control of the church. The charismatic movement has attracted many new believers at a time when affiliation with religious institutions is on the rise. Even churches with a more traditional worship service are meeting the needs of Cubans who seek spiritual nourishment but feel more comfortable with a more structured service and an opportunity for deeper theological reflection, rather than a highly emotive experience.

However, the question remains as to whether the doctrinal changes in the second rise of the revival have moved outside the Wesleyan tradition. The following chapter will review John and Charles Wesley's evangelical revival and draw some parallels with today's Cuban revival.

FOOTNOTES

84   Sterling Augustus Neblett, *Methodism's First Fifty Years in Cuba*, Wilmore, KY: Asbury Press, 1976, p.6.
85   *Disciplina de la Iglesia Metodista en Cuba*, p.V, Conferencia General, Marzo de 1991.
86   Neblett, p.6.
87   Ibid.
88   Ibid, p.8.
89   Ibid, p.9.
90   Ibid.
91   Ibid, p.17.
92   Ibid, p.18.
93   Ibid, p.19.
94   Ibid.

95   Ibid.

96   *La Disciplina de la Iglesia Metodista en Cuba*, p. V.

97   Ibid, p.VI.

98   Ibid.

99   Carlos Pérez, *Un Resumen de los Setenta Anos de Labor de la Iglesia Metodista en Cuba*, Miami: self-published, 1983, p.46.

100 Clyde W. Taylor, *Protestant Missions in Latin America: A Statistical Survey*, Washington: Evangelical Foreign Missions Association, 1961, p.110.

101 Telephone conversation with Dr. Larry Rankin, April 17, 1998.

102 Wingeier-Rayo and Chilcote, p.213.

103 Malone, p.2.

104 Interview with Bishop Armando Rodríguez, Sr., in Des Plaines, Illinois, January 20, 1998.

105 Ibid.

106 Ibid.

107 Taylor, p.110.

108 As John Wesley reflected on the early stages of Methodism, he used the term "rise" to refer to the first, second and third "rises" of Methodism in Oxford, Georgia, and London, respectively.

109 Interview with Bishop Joel Ajo in Racine, Wisconsin, April 8, 1998.

110 Ibid.

111 Interview with Bishop Armando Rodríguez, Sr. in Des Plaines, Illinois, January 20, 1998.

112 Ibid.

113 Ibid.

114 Ibid.

115 Interview with Rev. Emilio González in Zolfo Springs, Florida, March 21, 1998. My translation.

116 Ibid. My translation.

117 Ibid.

118 Ibid. My translation.

119 Conversation with Armando Rodríguez, Jr., March 17, 1998.

120 Interview with Bishop Joel Ajo in Racine, Wisconsin, April 8, 1998.

121 Interview with Rev. Emilio González in Zolfo Springs, Florida, March 21, 1998.

122 Interview with Bishop Joel Ajo in Racine, Wisconsin, April 8, 1998. My translation.

123 Ibid.

124 *Las Obras de Wesley* were finally translated into Spanish by the

Wesleyan Heritage Foundation, Justo González, General Editor, 1998.

125 Guido Benazet, *Una Paloma Blanca sobre una Isla Llamada Cuba*, Hialeah, Florida: Editorial A White Dove, 1994, p.50.

126 Ibid, p.49. My translation.

127 Interview with Bishop Armando Rodríguez, Sr. in Des Plaines, Illinois, January 20, 1998.

128 Ibid.

129 Benazet, p.56-7. My translation.

130 Ibid, p.58.

131 Ibid, p.59.

132 Ibid, p.58. My translation.

133 Wingeier-Rayo and Chilcote, p.208

134 Interview with Rev. Emilio González in Zolfo Springs, Florida, March 21, 1998.

135 Interview with Bishop Joel Ajo in Racine, Wisconsin, April 8, 1998.

136 Ibid.

137 Ibid.

138 Personal notes.

139 Interview with Bishop Joel Ajo in Racine, Wisconsin, April 8, 1998.

140 *El Evangelista Cubano, Tomo* 59, No. 3, December 1993, p.7.

141 Benazet, p.61. My translation.

142 Interview with Bishop Armando Rodríguez, Sr. in Des Plaines, Illinois, January 20, 1998.

143 Ibid.

144 IMECU, *"Pastoral para tiempos de crisis,"* Guido Benazet, *Una Paloma Blanca sobre una Isla Llamada Cuba*, p.77. My translation.

145 *"Documento sobre El Espiritu Santo en La Iglesia Metodista en Cuba," Conferencia Annual de la IMECU*, 1993, p.2. My translation.

146 Ibid. My translation.

147 Personal notes.

148 Sixth General Conference, March 1995.

149 Fifth Extraordinary Session of General Conference, March 1994.

150 Interview with Rev. Emilio González in Zolfo Springs, Florida, March 21, 1998. My translation.

151 Personal notes.

152 Personal notes.

153 Personal notes.

154 Kennedy, p. 20.

155 http://www.umc.org/umn3/story

CHAPTER V
A Comparison: Early Methodism and Cuban Methodism

John Wesley's 18th-Century Revival

The Church of England was in a state of decline at the beginning of the 18th century. Two major departures of clergy a few years earlier had weakened the church. First, in 1662, a large number of clergy were ejected from the Church of England for refusing to use the *Book of Common Prayer*. This was a group of Puritans to which John Wesley's maternal grandfather had belonged. In 1689, another group of clergy refused to give their oath of allegiance to the new royal family in England and were expelled as "non-jurors." Both expulsions occurred within a relatively short period of time, thus leaving the church with few qualified clergy and a lack of leadership."[156]

This double expulsion severely handicapped the church's ability to respond to the needs of the people at the dawn of the Industrial Revolution. The mechanization of mass production had begun, and thousands were moving from the countryside to the cities in hopes of finding a better life. Yet the expulsions had severely handicapped the church's ability to respond to the needs of the people at the dawn of the Industrial Revolution. Neither the country nor the church was ready for such a rapid demographic change, creating many social problems in urban areas. Inadequate housing, overpopulation, poor working conditions, and alcoholism were just a few of the problems that emerged in the cities.

The Church of England had become a church of the affluent and was unconcerned with the plight of the poor. Due to their lack of vision and empathy, church leaders made little effort to adapt their ministry to the changing context. Religion, as well as all aspects of life, had become very rational. After all, this was the height of the era of Enlightenment, which emphasized the use of reason and downplayed emotion. Wesley himself was the product of an educational system that was highly rational. Wesley was a graduate of Oxford University, the same great university that had produced John Locke, the philosophical deist, a century before.

When John Wesley's effort for spiritual renewal within the mother church evolved into a revival movement in the year 1739, it was not his intention to begin a new denomination but only to reform his beloved church. To his death Wesley was faithful to the Church of England and remained opposed to schism. "The design of Methodism," observed Samuel Christophers, "as its founder shows, is not to erect itself into a 'new sect,' or to build itself into a complete church fabric; but rather to 'reform the nation, particularly the church; and to spread Scriptural holiness over the land,' and through the world."[57]

As his ministry expanded, David Lowes Watson notes, "church order and doctrine became less important to Wesley than reaching out to 'the sinners in Cornwall, the keelmen in New Castle, the colliers in Kingswood and Staffordshire, the drunkards, the swearers, the Sabbath-breakers of Moorfield, and the harlots of Drury Lane.'"[58] As he preached, he enlisted followers into organized discipleship groups known as societies, classes and bands. "I soon found they were too many for me to talk with severally so often as they wanted it," he confessed. "So I told them, 'if you will all of you come together every Thursday in the evening, I will gladly spend some time with you in prayer, and give you the best advice I can."[159] The important point is that in spite of the growing differences between Wesley's renewal movement and the Anglican Church, he never advocated separation.

Although Wesley's early emphasis was on renewal, the Holy Spirit added the ingredient of revival that no one could have anticipated. During the Methodist gatherings there were unusual physical manifestations such as shaking, crying, screaming and fainting. Unsympathetic observers ridiculed this behavior and called the Wesley followers "enthusiasts."[160] Wesley himself was unsure how to react to these manifestations. He recorded in his journal some of the experiences he observed:

"Immediately one, and another, and another sunk to the earth: They dropped on every side as thunderstruck. One of them cried aloud. We besought God in her behalf, and He turned her heaviness into joy. A second being in the same agony, we called upon God for her also; and He spoke peace unto her soul . . ."[161]

"All Newgate rang with the cries of those whom the word of God cut to the heart; two of whom were in a moment filled with joy, to the astonishment of those that beheld them . . ."[162]

"A Quaker, who stood by, was not a little displeased at the dissimulation of those creatures, and was biting his lips and knitting his brows, when he dropped down as thunderstruck. The agony he was in was even terrible to behold. We besought God not to lay folly to his charge. And he soon lifted up his head, and cried aloud, now I know thou art a prophet of the Lord . . ."[163]

"Just as we rose from giving thanks, another person reeled four or five steps, and then dropped down. We prayed with her, and left her strongly convinced of sin, and earnestly groaning for deliverance . . ."[164]

Given the rational context of the Enlightenment Era, Wesley was careful to examine the persons experiencing these manifestations, so he asked them to return the following day for an interview.[165] He determined that all the people were of sound physical and emotional health and had not had any previous instances of unusual behavior or seizures. He also concluded that some had gone home justified of their sins and the rest were waiting patiently for it.[166] He placed great reliance on the observations of a doctor who had witnessed this phenomenon:

"We understand that many were offended at the cries of those on whom the power of God came; among whom was a physician, who was much afraid, there might be fraud or imposture in the case. Today one whom he had known many years, was the first (while I was preaching in Newgate) who broke out 'into strong cries and tears.' He could hardly believe his own eyes and ears. He went and stood close to her, and observed every symptom, till great drops of sweat ran down her face, and all her bones shook. He then knew not what to think, being clearly convinced it was not fraud, nor any natural disorder. But when both her soul and body were healed in a moment, he acknowledged the finger of God."[167]

Wesley was still unsure of the source of these unusual manifestations. Placing his primary authority for interpreting the experiences on Scripture, Wesley was uneasy about condemning them:

"I told them, they were not to judge of the spirit whereby any one spoke either by appearances, or by common report, or by their own inward feelings: No, nor by any dreams, visions or revelations, supposed to be made to their souls; any more than by their tears, or any involuntary effects wrought upon their bodies. I warned them, all these were, in themselves, of a doubtful, disputable nature; they might be from God, and they might not; and were therefore not simply to be relied on, (any more than simply to be condemned,) but to be tried by a farther rule, to be brought to the only certain test, the Law and the Testimony."[168]

Wesley's religious upbringing in an Anglican home had not included any such experiences. However, following Wesley's evangelical conversion on May 24, 1738, he became a staunch supporter of the doctrine of faith of assurance. He recorded in his diary, "I felt my heart strangely warmed. I felt I did trust in Christ, Christ alone for salvation; and an assurance was given me that He had taken away my sins, even mine, and saved me from the law of sin and death."[169] This experience strengthened Wesley's ability to evaluate these manifestations in terms of their contribution to a faith of assurance.

Wesley differentiated between the ordinary gifts of the Spirit—love, joy, peace, patience, kindness, goodness, fidelity, gentleness and self-control— and the extraordinary gifts of healing, tongues, prophecy, discernment of spirits, and teaching. This distinction was helpful in interpreting whether or not these unusual physical manifestations led to the faith of assurance:

"I have seen (as far as a thing of this kind can be seen) very many persons changed in a moment from the spirit of fear, horror, despair, to the spirit of love, joy, peace; and from sinful desire, till then reigning over them, to a pure desire of doing the will of God. These are matters of fact, where of I have been, and almost daily am, an eye or ear witness. What I have to say vouching visions or dreams, is this: I know several persons in whom this great change was wrought in dream, or during a strong representation to the eye of their mind, of Christ either on the cross, or in glory. This is the fact; let any judge of it as they please. And that such a change was then wrought, appears (not from their shedding tears only, or falling into fits, or crying out: These are not the fruits, as you seem to suppose, whereby I judge, but) from the whole tenor of their life, till then, many ways wicked; from that time, holy, just and good."[170]

In other words, the physical reaction in itself was not proof of conversion. Rather, Wesley was careful to look beyond that experience to see the ensuing results of peace, joy, love, conviction of sin, liberty and praise for God with the faith of assurance.

Wesley was wise enough not to assume he could explain what influences might cause a body to undergo such sudden and sharp awakenings. However, he did indicate that "Satan" could take advantage of these physical manifestations in order to hinder, confuse or distract converts: "But I make no question that Satan, so far as he gets power, may exert himself on such occasions, partly to hinder the good work in the persons who are thus touched with the sharp arrows of conviction, and partly to disparage the work of God, as if it tended to lead people to distraction."[171] Although these manifestations could be a by-product of a faith of assurance, they could also be used by Satan to scare people away from God.

Wesley's openness to a variety of new birth experiences was secondary in importance to the ensuing step of discipleship. His creation of the societies, classes and bands provided accountability in his followers' journey toward greater spiritual holiness. His ideas concerning small discipleship groups came from the primitive church and the Moravian Pietists, and exemplified the ancient tradition of devotion to "the apostles' teaching and fellowship, to the breaking of bread and the prayers."

(Acts 2:42)

Wesley's organizational genius was to structure his followers into an institution where they could be empowered, as well as nurtured, in their faith. Although the original purpose of class meetings, for example, was to raise money to pay for the chapel at Bristol, Wesley quickly discovered how these covenant groups could be used to promote and encourage mutual accountability.[172] Summarized succinctly in the words of David Lowes Watson, the societies, classes, and bands were "structures for discipleship and mission."[173]

An important aspect of holiness was the "love of neighbor." The early Methodist "Holy Club" took up a weekly offering to help prison inmates and their families. In addition, the Methodist movement started schools and dispensaries.[174] Wesley even wrote a pharmaceutical book with home remedies for common illnesses. While John and Charles Wesley and their colleagues carried out these social ministries, "they saw their primary task as preaching the gospel."[175] But they and the early Methodists were also concerned about meeting the material needs of people.

One of the common signs of church renewal is the rediscovery of Scripture. The Bible was John Wesley's first language as he grew up in the Epworth rectory, where his parents shared daily devotions and encouraged the reading of the Bible. In fact, it is well known that Wesley described himself as a *"homo unius libri"* (man of one book).[176] It is not surprising that Wesley intentionally shaped his message around focal themes of scripture and his thorough knowledge of the biblical text. In the words of Albert Outler, "Wesley lived in the Scriptures and his mind ranged over the Bible's length and breadth and depth like a radar, tuned into the pertinent data on every point he cared to make."[177] The Wesleyan renewal movement was a rediscovery of the living Word.

It was also characterized by the active participation of lay men and women in its leadership. As the societies and class meetings began to spread, Wesley found it necessary to rely upon class leaders to nurture his followers toward spiritual maturity. Receiving little support and encouragement from the ordained clergy, he was willing to use lay people who might further his cause. Stressing in his theology that each individual has value to God and that God meets everyone where he or she is, Wesley was able to empower common people for positions of leadership in his movement. These leaders were normally laymen or women, neither ordained clergy nor Methodist itinerant preachers, and very often of humble origin with little or no education.[178]

Detailed analysis of early Methodist class lists also reveals the fact that women outnumbered men by a ratio of two to one.[179] The role of these class leaders, male and female alike, was extremely important within the life of the growing societies and in the quest for spiritual maturity among the Methodist people.

The class and band meetings within the Methodist societies were essentially small groups of believers who met together for the purpose of accountable discipleship. These were house groups in which Methodists encouraged one another in the faith. In Wesley's words, a society was ". . . a company of men [and women] having the form and seeking the power of godliness, united in order to pray together, to receive the Word of exhortation, and to watch over one another in love, that they may help each other work out their salvation."[180]

The class leaders would ask the members questions such as, "How is it with your soul?" "What sin have you committed since last week?" "What temptations and victories have you experienced?" "Do you want to keep anything secret?" "Have you God's forgiveness of your sins?"[181] The purpose of these intimate questions was to hold individuals accountable in their growth toward maturity, or what Wesley often described as "perfect love." Accountable discipleship led to maturity of faith and holy living. Thus, the ministry of the laity was absolutely fundamental to the growth and maintenance of the Wesleyan renewal movement.

The Wesleyan movement was also characterized by the rediscovery of the classical spiritual disciplines. These included prayer, fasting, the Word (read, heard, and meditated upon), Christian conference or fellowship, and the Eucharist, or sacrament of Holy Communion. These disciplines are referred to by Wesley as "the means of grace." Liturgical renewal, which conjoins these disciplines with the rediscovery of vital faith, is well illustrated in the evangelical revival. In Wesley's case this took the specific shape of a rediscovery of the Eucharist. He encouraged his followers to attend their local Anglican parish churches and participate in their sacramental life, even to the point of exhorting their priests to a more frequent celebration of the sacrament.

The Wesleys reintroduced Love Feasts, Watch Night services or vigils, and opportunities for covenant renewal into the common round of Christian worship. More important than any of these innovations, however, was their rediscovery of congregational singing, especially through the ministry of Charles Wesley. Methodism, one might say, was born in song, and Wesleyan hymns revolutionized worship.

The Renewal of Cuban Methodism

The Methodist Church in Cuba, like the Wesleyan Revival of 18th-century England, is also enjoying a challenging moment of change, and some of the parallels are striking. It has been a long and difficult road for Cuban Methodism, however, to get to where it is today. There have been major losses of pastors and church leaders. The first exodus followed the 1961 announcement of President Fidel Castro on the eve of the Bay of Pigs invasion that the Revolution was socialist. The attitude of the government toward the church at that time became antagonistic, and many people believed that Christianity had no future in Cuba. Of the 51 Cuban Methodist pastors, 43 left the country in the first few years of the Revolution, not to mention the 54 U.S. missionaries who were also recalled at that time.

In 1980, however, the opening up of the Mariel boatlift created a second mass exodus, this time of more than 125,000 Cubans. The church was not exempt from this emigration; the Methodist Church lost four seminary-trained pastors. One consequence of this second exodus was the fact that there was no qualified person left to succeed Bishop Armando Rodríguez, who served his episcopacy from 1968 to 1990, as General Conference

An occupied Methodist parsonage (beside church) in the town of Jovellanos.

continued to elect him until his retirement. In that extremely oppressive environment, the government confiscated the homes of all the "*gusanos*" (traitors)[182] and for the church this meant losing several parsonages. In other cases, needy families simply began squatting in vacant chapels or parsonages. In spite of the great effort of some dedicated lay people to protect church property and replace their pastors, the loss of leadership resulting from these two important events created a void which the church is only now beginning to fill.

The lack of experienced and well-trained Methodist pastors has made the tensions around church growth even greater. In 1989 the second rise of the revival intensified and many people have been converted to Christ since then. Many of these Methodist neophytes are youth between the ages of 15 and 30 who are very enthusiastic about their faith. The worship style and theology of these new converts is very different from that of the traditional lifelong Methodists.

One might think that with the tide of young people into this expanding renewal movement, and with a large influx of previously unchurched young people, they might have a desire to start their own church. Their innovative forms of worship, so unlike those of the traditional Methodist Church, would seem to warrant a move in that direction. In addition, there has been staunch opposition to these charismatic manifestations from the more traditional sector of the church, although the renewal movement has remained inside the existing structures of the church.

Facing the threats of schism, Rev. Emilio González's voice for unity prevailed following the 1995 General Conference. Ironically, the control of the Cuban government prevents schism anyway by prohibiting the establishment of any new denominations in Cuba. In addition, this movement, on the whole, has learned to have more love and understanding for those in opposition. This is the lesson that was learned from the failure of Ariel González's movement in 1974.[183] The revival has been successful in renewal because it has stayed within the existing denomination and significantly affected the Methodist Church in Cuba.

Many unusual physical manifestations have occurred in the movement, beginning with the supernatural smell of perfume experienced by Rev. Emilio González. Speaking in tongues, being "slain in the Spirit," and discernment of the spirits have all been observed at extension classes for pastors, youth assemblies, and local churches. The many new converts have been encouraged to participate in a congregation. In towns and communities where there was no sanctuary, house churches have been established to offer worship services, Bible studies, and a support community. The Methodist Church in Cuba has opened 200 house churches during the past ten years.[184]

This Cuban revival movement is characterized by a deep faith in God during very uncertain times. Shortages of food and material goods have meant that people are working literally for today's supper. The changing situation from day to day has meant that young people have little hope for their future. The people who are converted to Jesus Christ are living by faith. Testimonies of the recent converts express gratitude to God for food that was provided in a moment of shortage, or medicine that appeared during a time of illness, or a bus that allowed them to come to church. The revival in Cuba is characterized by a living faith that is simple and practical.

Another characteristic of the movement is a return to the Scriptures. For nearly three decades it was very difficult to acquire Bibles. Since 1979, however, the

United Bible Society has been shipping Bibles through Mexico to Cuba. The greatly increased availability of the Word of God in the 1990s has meant that young people who never had access to a Bible are able to read it on their own. Eager to seek a new foundation for their future, the recent converts study the Scripture with great zeal. It is not uncommon for Methodist churches to have services four or five nights a week. The worship services include readings from the Old and New Testaments, and then a sermon about the passage. These are signs that the revival movement takes the Word of God seriously, placing it at the center of church life.

Like its early Methodist antecedent, the revival movement in contemporary Cuba is fueled by the active participation of lay people. Not only are the lay leaders attending to the new missions and house churches, but they are also active in leading the worship services in the main churches. Their participation is crucial to the maintenance and expansion of the church at the grassroots level. At the annual conference level, however, their participation is somewhat stifled by a structure of power dominated by the longtime clergy and lay leadership.

Nevertheless, it is exciting to see how the lay people have kept alive many churches and started new missions. Although some have attended training classes, very few have had any formal theological training. They begin and maintain house churches in remote areas where there are insufficient itinerant pastors to fill the need. When the ordained clergy were sent to cut sugar cane in the Military Units for Production (U.M.A.P.), the pastors' wives and other lay men and women took charge of the churches, and not one church was closed as a result of the government's policy.[185] It is really the lay people who have sustained the church in Cuba and who have assumed leadership positions in the revival movement.

These lay people seek out a community of worship to nourish their faith through the practice of accountable discipleship. These groups are not nearly as disciplined as during Wesley's time, but they offer people opportunities to encourage one another. The house churches serve as one arena in which members of a community can share their testimonies and exhort one another in the faith. This is not an intimate setting, however, where one can be honest about one's sins and temptations. The lack of freedom of expression in Cuba has been internalized, and this breaks down trust in a public setting. While disciples are willing to share intimately with a neighbor or church member, they are less likely to place themselves in a vulnerable position in a public service, even in the intimacy of a home.

The rediscovery of the Bible is central to the Cuban Methodist revival. Young people who have been educated in atheist schools are hungry for the Word of God. Initially they are neophytes, but they are eager to study the Bible. All churches include Bible study as one of their weekly programs. Due to the eagerness of a new convert to read the Bible at home and multiple weekday services at church, a new Christian learns a lot of Scripture in a relatively short period of time. In addition to the greater availability of Bibles in churches, it is also a best-seller at state-run bookstores.

Prayer is another spiritual discipline that is absolutely central to the renewal movement in Cuba. Prayer is practiced alone, in small groups, and in the context of corporate worship. People feel that prayer is essential in order to be in greater communion with God. On occasion the leaders of the movement will hold a prayer vigil in which the young people will be encouraged to seek the extraordinary gifts of the Spirit, such as speaking in tongues, healing, prophecy, discernment, and teaching.

The understanding is that through spiritual disciplines such as prayer and fasting, one can seek the baptism of the Holy Spirit, including the extraordinary gifts of the Spirit.

Fellowship, or Christian conferencing, as Wesley called it, comes naturally to the Cuban revival. Because the Cuban culture is very communal and social, it is normal for a community of believers to gather together on a regular basis to pray, read the Bible, culminate their fast, and then break their fast together.[186] In addition, it is important to have the support and encouragement of fellow Christians, since being a Christian is still despised by many in the Cuban context.

Of all the spiritual disciplines, fasting was the most neglected by the traditional church in Cuba.[187] The revival has rescued this Christian practice and made it central in each local church.[188] One day a week each congregation is encouraged to fast, and a fasting service is held at their church either in the morning or at noon to offer the fast to God. These services are very popular with house churches because they are community-based and accessible to the members. Oftentimes, after the house church has culminated a fast, they will break the fast together with some coffee and cake. These practices have awakened the larger church to the importance of the discipline of fasting.

The shortage of ordained clergy has meant that the Eucharist has not been celebrated as frequently as in Wesley's day. This is a divergence from early Methodist practice, which included an emphasis on this means of grace. However, it is common for house churches to conclude with a coffee hour (see previous page). This could be interpreted symbolically as "breaking bread" with the community of faith. In addition churches celebrate a love feast every December 31 as a service of thanksgiving for having completed the year. This festive evening involves typical Cuban *criollo* food with yucca, pork, rice and black beans, and concludes with a worship service renewing their covenant with God for the coming year. In spite of these practices, after the exodus of Cuban pastors, the church has not maintained the same Wesleyan emphasis on the Eucharist.

In 1994 Armando Rodríguez Jr. wrote a thesis entitled *"Compartamos el Pan y el Vino"* ("Let's Share the Bread and Wine"), documenting the infrequency of communion and exhorting the church to make it more readily available. The following year, the General Conference changed *The Book of Discipline* to allow local pastors to celebrate the Eucharist in their local churches, thus moving the Cuban church closer to historical Methodism.

The economic shortages and isolation of Cuba have also affected church practices. The traditional North American liturgy is being replaced by a more contextualized Cuban worship style. Since paper is scarce and most churches do not have access to a photocopier, bulletins are rare and services are not restricted by a printed order of worship. The hymnals brought by the missionaries in pre-Castro Cuba, along with *The Book of Worship*, have been lost, eaten by termites or used for toilet paper, freeing pastors to create the order of worship. Most rely on the Bible or materials acquired in extension courses to plan worship, but the lack of standard guidelines can create variations in denominational practice. It is not uncommon to have neighboring churches worship in entirely different styles, both calling themselves Methodists.

The worship style of these new converts is enthusiastic, which is consistent with Cuban idiosyncrasy and culture. They enjoy rhythmic, uplifting contemporary music. Pianos, before the availability of electronic key-

Praise band with native instruments in town of Belic.

boards, were usually in disrepair, and so popular Cuban instruments such as guitars, tambourines, and bongo drums are used for worship.[189] Traditional hymns are gradually being replaced by praise songs which are easy to remember. Armando Rodríguez Jr. commented: "Anyone who knows a little about our current liturgical celebrations knows that they have experienced an evident renewal through the introduction of the so-called choruses or praise songs."[190] The worship service has a festive, celebrative feel.

The liturgical renewal was not without resistance from the older, more traditional members of the congregation. Sometimes the older members silently protested by not standing up and clapping to the praise music. At other times their protest was channeled through the local administrative board of the church. According to the rules in *The Book of Discipline*, election to church offices required two years as a member. New arrivals did not qualify and therefore were not represented in the administrative board meetings.

Initially, loud enthusiastic worship services were reprimanded by the old guard. Eventually, however, the young members were elected to the administrative board, and their energy and enthusiasm were contagious. These struggles occurred in local churches across the island until eventually the older members found themselves in the minority and relinquished their positions. Some voluntarily joined the enthusiastic form of worship, while most were labeled as "obsolete" and resigned themselves to the new way of worship.

In Wesley's time, the means of grace combined both works of piety and works of mercy. Similarly in Cuba, the youth enthusiastically affirm the interrelation of prayer and social service. On their own initiative these young Christians reach out to others in hospitals, jails, boarding schools, and private homes. They truly believe that God loves everyone, even the poor and uneducated. Most of their evangelization occurs among the marginalized people of Cuban society. While the Cuban government will not allow the church to have its own social service agencies, except for nursing homes, those in the renewal movement focus their energy on individual works of mercy toward those in need wherever they may be found.

Similarities and Differences

Although the 18th-century evangelical revival in England took place in a very different context from the one presently occurring in Cuban Methodism, there are some very intriguing parallels.

Both societies placed more emphasis on the use of reason than on the emotions. Wesley's movement was set in the midst of Europe's Era of Enlightenment, while the revival in Cuba occurred in the context of materialist philosophies imported from Soviet-style Marxism-Leninism, with little attention to the emotional and spiritual aspects of the human being.

In addition, both churches experienced a critical loss of leadership in the years preceding the emergence of the renewal movement, and both reflect the uncertainties of social upheaval. Although Wesley's societies, classes, and bands were much more structured and intimate than the house churches in Cuba today, both movements reflect concern for accountable discipleship and serious spiritual formation.

Neither movement arose for the purpose of establishing a separate church; rather, both had the sole intent of renewing their denomination. Both movements have received their strength by reclaiming the classical spiritual disciplines— by engaging in Bible study, prayer, fellowship, and fasting, the relative unavailability of the Eucharist to Cuban Methodists making communion the one exception. Using Wesley's 18th-century renewal movement as a guide, even the casual observer will discern the emergence within the Methodist Church in Cuba of a legitimate revival along the lines of the Wesleyan tradition.

The two movements, however, have some striking differences as well. Wesley stood at the forefront of his movement as a charismatic leader of great stature and wide-ranging influence. In Cuba, although Bishop Pereira is a very commanding figure and the undisputed leader of the charismatic movement today, many lesser-known leaders initiated the first and second rises of the revival.

Most of the people entering the societies in England were baptized Anglicans, while in Cuba the overwhelming majority of the new people have come from atheist or non-Christian backgrounds, with the exception of a few who had been baptized in the Catholic Church. The revival movement began in Cuba among lifelong Methodists, but in recent years it has expanded beyond the baptized to take in many members from secular society. This has meant an increase in adult baptisms and a great need for training and practice in discipleship.

Due to Cuba's isolation during the 1960s and '70s, the leaders of the revival movement did not have access to classical theological, historical, and liturgical study that would have brought them closer to church tradition. While extension courses were given to new pastors, few pastors had access to full-time theological preparation.

The extension courses were delivered through *encuentros* (meetings) in which the pastors were summoned three times a year for a five-day workshop. The classes were taught by the few remaining Methodist pastors who had graduated from the seminary. One major impediment was the shortage of textbooks.[191] Although these *encuentros* provided some theological background, it was not nearly as rigorous or as extensive as a four-year seminary program.

To make matters worse, during the 1970s and '80s Bishop Armando Rodríguez disagreed with the pro-government tendencies of the Seminario Evangelico de Teologia, where Methodist pastors traditionally have been trained. The longtime rector of the seminary, Dr. Sergio Arce, was a proponent of "Theology in Revolution" which was supportive of the government. Therefore, under Bishop Rodríguez, the Methodist Church did not send students to be trained there for several years. Joel Ajo was the last Methodist graduate of the seminary in 1974 until Rinaldo Hernández, Jr. insisted upon attending and graduated in 1988.

As a result, many Cuban pastors had to rely upon Scripture and experience to inform their theology, while lacking greater development in the areas of Christian tradition and reason. This lack of emphasis on theological education stands in contrast to Wesley's knowledge of church tradition and the bibliography that he required each Methodist preacher to read.

There are also political differences between the Wesley revival in 18th-century England and the Cuban revival today. Although both countries were facing social upheaval, Wesley was a Tory who favored the British crown, while the Cuban Methodist leadership is in favor of change. John Wesley believed that the king of England was ordained by God to govern England.[192] Wesley had observed rebellions against the monarchy in English and European contexts and did not see any positive changes as a result. Personally, Wesley was the victim of some of the mob violence generated by civil unrest. This is one reason why he considered popular rule as tantamount to anarchy.[193] The opinions of the Cuban Methodist leadership differ from Wesley in that they favor a republic.

Another area where a divergence can be seen is social service. While analyzing this difference one must take into account different social contexts. Wesley's movement enjoyed the freedom to start schools and dispensaries in 18th-century England. In Cuba, however, the government still does not allow any private health care and education providers. The only aspect of social services open to the church is assisted living nursing homes for older adults.

Following the visits of Joan Campbell of the National Council of Churches (U.S.A.) and Pastors for Peace in 1991 and 1992, the Cuban church became a common channel of international aid. But since the government was in charge of all health care, the church donated these medicines to state-run clinics and hospitals. In the eyes of the government, this raised the visibility and prestige of the church, and older Christians saw it as vindication for ill-treatment during the 1960s and '70s.

Cuban Pastor Daniel Williams (right) and U.M. missionary Diana Wingeier-Rayo (center) deliver medicines to a clinic in town of Punta Brava.

Press releases in government newspapers interpreted these donations as signs of church support for government policies. Reactionary Christians, wanting to distance themselves from the government, feared that the press releases could be manipulated by the government to produce a pro-Castro image. For example, in recent years the Methodist Church has avoided partnerships with the state for fear of being associated with the state.

Shawn Malone at Georgetown University's Cuba Project explains this phenomenon among evangelical denominations in Cuba: "Charismatic and evangelical churches, on the other hand, have often emphasized evangelization and spiritual development, focusing their efforts on maintaining space for pastoral ministry and attempting to distance themselves from political issues."[194] This does not preclude all Protestants from social service, as other denominations have social ministries, but certainly the Methodist Church as a national institution is involved in very few social services.

In spite of this generalization, the national church

does have a beautiful nursing home in Havana which provides hospice care for the elderly. In a creative partnership with the government, the Methodist Church refurbished an old mansion into assisted living quarters, while the state provided the salaries for health care professionals. The program is directed by Rev. Doralbis Hidalgo and offers both internal and outpatient services. Initially open to anyone, the limited space is now filled to capacity by longtime Methodists and their family members.

In addition, there are some cases in which Methodist Churches at the local level have started ministries to benefit the community. For example, the Marianao church in Havana has an effective prison ministry that offers the inmates both spiritual and material assistance. The church in Aguada de Pasajeros has equipped a local hospital with medical supplies. The Santa Clara church has a ministry with HIV/AIDS patients at the state-run sanatorium. The Methodist Church in Playa Manteca has a community garden that provides vegetables for the congregation, public school and day care center. But in general, while many new converts are filled with great love for their fellow citizens and express individual acts of kindness, there are few organized institutional ministries to address social issues.

In another area, both the Wesleyan revival in 18th-century England and the Cuban revival have experienced manifestations of the Holy Spirit. Each movement was uncertain as to how to discern the origin of these experiences, and both have been criticized by the traditional sector that did not understand such manifestations. In England, Methodists were ridiculed as "enthusiasts," while Cubans today are called "fanatics." Both movements also have looked to the fruits of conversion or the ordinary gifts of the spirit to confirm the legitimacy of these extraordinary gifts.

However, the similarities between each movement's doctrine of the Holy Spirit end there. Wesley's movement was grounded in a much more solid theological teaching which emphasized the faith of assurance, whereas in the Cuban charismatic movement some sectors looked to the physical manifestations as evidence of a deeper faith. Although it is impossible to generalize, some leaders in the second stage of the Cuban revival do approve of falling as a visual sign of being close to God. While Wesley believed that this one-time experience could lead to new birth, he never advocated subsequent experiences, such as repetitive falling in the search for spiritual gifts. Moreover, he cautioned that scandalous manifestations could be used as "Satan's instrument" to frighten people away from God.

John Wesley has been described by Albert Outler as a folk theologian who was eclectic in his combination of theological motifs. He was a scholar in the classics of the church fathers and drew initially on Anglicanism, Catholicism, Pietism, Mysticism, Puritanism and the Moravians. Once the Methodist revival began in 1738, however, he became highly consumed by the supervision of the movement and had less and less opportunity to observe other movements. Wesley was open to Quakers, Baptists and other non-conformists visiting the Methodist societies, but as the movement consolidated it became more self-sufficient.

The Cuban movement differs on this score, in that it has had more ongoing dialogue with religious movements from other traditions—particularly with Pentecostal and interdenominational groups from abroad—while the Wesleyan movement became more inwardly focused.

FOOTNOTES

156   Rupert E. Davies. *Methodism*, London: Epworth Press, 1985, p.25.

157   Samuel Christophers, Class *Meetings in Relation to the Design and Success of Methodism*, London: Wesleyan Conference Office, 1873, p.33.

158   David Lowes Watson, *Covenant Discipleship*, Nashville: Discipleship Resources, 1989, p.51.

159   Christophers, p.19.

160   Stephen Gunter, *The Limits of Love Divine: John Wesley's Response to Antinomianism and Enthusiasm*, Nashville: Kingswood, 1979, p.23.

161   Ibid, p.188.

162   Ibid, p.189.

163   *Wesley's Works, Vol.I*, p.190.

164   Ibid, p.190.

165   Ibid, p.204.

166   Ibid.

167   Ibid, p.189.

168   Ibid, p.206.

169   *Journal, Vol. I*, pp.475-76.

170   *Works, Vol.I*, p.195.

171   Ibid, p.208.

172   Joseph Willis, *The Class and the Congregation of Wesleyan Methodism*, London: Elliot Stock, 1869, p.22.

173   Watson, p.51.

174   Richard Heitzenrater, *Wesley and the People Called Methodists*, Nashville: Abingdon Press, 1995, p.126.

175   Ibid, p.125.

176   *Letters, III*, "Letter to William Dodd," p.156.

177   Albert Outler, *Theology in the Wesleyan Spirit*, Nashville: Discipleship Resources, 1975, p.11.

178   Davies, p.63.

179   Paul W. Chilcote, *She Offered Them Christ*, Nashville: Abingdon Press, 1993, p.26.

180   Christophers, p.23.

181   Mortimer Arias, "Methodist Societies in the Eighteenth Century and Christian Base Communities in the Twentieth Century," in Theodore Runyon, *Wesley Theology Today*, Nashville: Kingswood Books, 1985, p.236.

182   A Spanish word which literally means "worms," although Cubans use it as a derogatory term for those who fled the country, i.e. traitors.

183   Interview with Rev. Emilio González in Zolfo Springs, Florida, March 21, 1998.

184   Wingeier-Rayo and Chilcote, p.215.

185   Interview with Bishop Armando Rodríguez, Sr., in Des Plaines, Illinois, January 20, 1998.

186   Wingeier-Rayo and Chilcote, p.220.

187   Benazet, p.76.

188   Ibid.

189   Armando Rodríguez, Jr., p.12. My translation.

190   Ibid.

191   Interview with Bishop Joel Ajo in Racine, Wisconsin, April 8, 1998.

192   John Wesley, "Thoughts concerning the origin of power," *Works, Vol.I*, p.51.

193   Ibid, p.53.

194   Malone, p.10.

CHAPTER VI

Conclusions and Observations

Summary

Although the Methodist Church in Cuba did not die, as biblical models of revival suggest, it faced extremely difficult conditions in the 1960s and '70s. Many people thought that the church in Cuba was an endangered species. Although some pastors and lay people prayed for a return to the pre-Castro church, the Revolution, collapse of the U.S.S.R., tightening of the U.S. embargo and ensuing economic crisis had produced a new context, requiring a "new wineskin." A revival emerged from the grassroots, borrowing some theology and worship styles along the way, to produce a movement which echoes biblical revivals.

In addition, the relationship between the church and the state warmed up considerably, producing favorable conditions for a revival. After work camps, property confiscation and persecution, which represented the state's treatment of the church in the 1960s, the late 1980s brought dialogue and even cooperation. Fidel Castro's encounters with progressive Christians throughout Latin America gave him a greater appreciation for Christianity's contributions to society.

Following the historic first meeting between Protestant leaders and Castro in 1990, church-state relations improved dramatically. Church leaders were given greater privileges, house churches were made legal, church agencies abroad were given greater opportunities to operate in Cuba. The Fourth Congress of the Communist Party in 1991 amended the constitution and struck down discriminatory barriers for believers.

After the former Soviet Union withdrew its subsidies, the state could no longer afford to alienate the growing religious sector within Cuba. Rekindling ties to Latin American countries, which tend to be very religious, and to liberal Christians in the West, Cuba tried to attract investment and humanitarian aid. The warming relationship between the church and the state thus contributed to conditions for a spiritual revival.

Inside the Methodist Church some pastors experimented with the gifts of the Holy Spirit and promoted changes in the liturgy. Praise songs with contemporary music and spontaneous informal services replaced the traditional worship style. The organs and pianos left by the missionaries were in disrepair and popular Cuban instruments like guitars, bongos, congas, claves, maracas and tambourines replaced them. Notwithstanding resistance from some pastors, the changes in Cuban worship style eventually spread throughout the denomination.

The revival occurred in two stages. The first rise was a quiet renewal within the Methodist clergy which began at pastors' meetings and extension courses. The second rise began in 1989 and extended beyond the Methodist Church. This phase involved greater interaction with Pentecostal and independent churches from inside and outside of Cuba.

In summary, the two rises of revival within Cuban Methodism echo biblical images of revival offered by the prophets in the post-exilic literature. The changes in Cuba also have similarities with the evangelical revival in 18th-century England, such as economic conditions, rapid social change, and a shortage of clergy theologically trained to address the people's needs. Laity were empowered to disciple new believers in small groups and address these needs in early Methodism and Cuban Methodism alike. Unusual physical manifestations occurred, and Wesley responded with suspicion and uncomfortable acceptance when justification and sanctification were evident.

A sector of Cuban Methodists embraced these manifestations, especially after outside influences taught a charismatic worship style and the doctrine of baptism of the Holy Spirit. While both Wesley's movement and Cuban Methodism lacked trained clergy, Wesley's rejection of doctrines that he considered harmful (predestination, quietism and entire instantaneous sanctification) established a clear Methodist doctrine, while Cuban Methodism preferred tolerance. Candidates for the ministry did not attend formal theological training in either setting, but Wesley required his "Christian Library," and Cuban Methodists required periodic *"encuentros."*

One significant difference between the movements was Wesley's support for the monarchy and the Cuban movement's uneasiness with the revolutionary government. Wesley's evangelical revival incorporated both the spiritual and social aspects of the gospel through schools, orphanages and health care, while Cuban Methodism has been limited to evangelical Christianity under a paternalistic socialist government. As the movements matured, Wesley relied more exclusively on resources from within while Cuban Methodism has formed partnerships outside the Wesleyan family.

Certainly it is unfair to compare two movements in such different cultures and political systems. However, in my opinion excessive outside influence can lead Cuban Methodism to extremes beyond the heritage of the people called Methodists.

A Mission of Accompaniment

A major part of my responsibility as a missionary assigned by the General Board of Global Ministries to the Methodist Church in Cuba was to act as a liaison between the Cuban and North American churches. The one-year exchange with Rev. Rinaldo Hernández was the first step in breaking down barriers of misunderstanding that had existed since the outset of the Revolution. Next, the bishop asked me to host travel seminars for others to come and learn about the Cuban context through hands-on visits to churches, schools, hospitals and state-run agencies.

The Cuban government balked, however, when we invited a work team from upstate New York to repair a church in San Juan de los Yeras in central Cuba in September of 1991. Dr. José Felipe Carneado asked Bishop Ajo, "Why do you need North Americans to work when we have so many Cubans in need of employment?"

While certainly understanding a valid point, Bishop Ajo responded in a language the government would understand: "It's not the work they do, rather it is the solidarity they express with the church and the Cuban people." Thus, the government approved the first work team on a trial basis. The team not only repaired the church roof, it also went across the street and painted the local elementary school, generally earning rave reviews and opening the door for future teams. I was later named coordinator of Volunteers in Mission in Cuba, beginning a new phase of my missionary responsibilities.

At the 1992 United Methodist General Conference in Louisville, Kentucky, I met Rev. Tom Curtis, then director of the Southeastern Jurisdiction's office of Volunteers in Mission. Together with Bishop Ajo we planned an initial exploration trip, to be followed by several building teams to repair churches and parsonages.

I often took these groups to visit the home of a long-time Methodist layperson, Ysel Pérez, to learn about the Cuban reality over a cup of Cuban coffee. She and her husband Orlando Rovira were members of the Methodist Church before the Revolution and were largely responsible for building University Methodist Church and protecting it from confiscation. Pérez had a unique family situation, for following her husband's death she lived with her son René, who married a woman named Miriam, a member of the Communist Party and an atheist.

This apparent ideological contradiction in a Christian home would often provoke visitors to ask,"Is it possible for a Christian to marry a Communist and get along?" René and Miriam were present at these meetings and they responded, "We don't see a contradiction, because we both have deep nationalist pride and want the best for Cuba." They obviously also wanted the best education and opportunities for their daughter Jenny. On those fre-

Isel Perez (seated, center) in her Havana apartment with son Rene and granddaughter Jenny (standing) and daughter-in-law Miriam (seated, left).

quent visits, Ysel Pérez became famous for her quote: "Cuba isn't heaven, but it isn't hell either."

The theme song for the Methodist revival is called: "*Cuba para Cristo*" (Cuba for Christ). The lyrics read:

> Christians are rising up, Christians are rising up,
> And now they are praying for you.
> We want your grace, we want your love,
> And soon we will be able to say:
> Cuba for Christ, Cuba for Christ,
> Christ is life, Christ is love,
> He will change my country and make it better.

The words of this song, which is sung at every church rally in Cuba, represent the church's hope that revival will produce a better homeland. When an individual or family accepts Jesus as their savior, they are rejecting the uncertainty and fatalism that pervades Cuban society and replacing it with faith in the God of life.

In the summer of 1994 Cuba faced its greatest crisis when more than 50,000 rafters risked their lives to cross the Florida straits. The economic crisis had reached dangerous heights that summer as food and transportation shortages had produced all-time lows. Power outages, by then a daily occurrence, lasted as long as 16 hours. Unable to use electric fans, many people placed their mattresses on their rooftops to escape the suffocating summer heat. No electricity meant no television or entertainment, which was an additional spark to an already irritable and volatile population. Observers compared the situation to a pressure cooker ready to explode. Frustration sparked mini-protests, crowds throwing rocks and bottles onto the street, but the worst was yet to come.

On July 13, a tugboat operator hijacked a boat called *Trece de Marzo* from the Havana harbor with 32 people aboard. Some Cuban naval boats caught up with the tugboat several miles off shore and sank it.[195] The events of that fateful day have not been clarified, and Cuban exiles continue to protest by organizing a yearly flotilla which travels from Miami to the site of the tragedy to throw wreaths to the victims.

This event triggered another explosive event on August 5 when a group of would-be emigrants shot and killed a police officer in an attempt to hijack a ferry from Havana harbor. As a crowd formed around Havana's Malecon street in the highly populated lower-class neighborhood of *Centro Habana*, people became rowdy and started throwing stones, breaking the windows of a tourist hotel and a dollar store.[196] Governmental "Immediate Action Brigades," an instrument of the state security apparatus, were deployed to disband the crowds.

The next day President Castro announced that Cuba would no longer use its police force to defend the United States' borders and would allow all who wished to leave the country freely. This was the escape valve to the pressure cooker.

This began a dramatic one-and-a-half-month exodus that would see approximately 50,000 Cubans attempt to emigrate on styrofoam rafts and inner tubes. An estimated 20,000 were lost at sea. Young people who were frustrated by the scarcities, tempted by images of abundance in the United States, and willing to brave the perilous journey across the Florida straits, decided that the gamble was worth it.

In the middle of this turbulence, when ordinary Cubans were ready to risk their lives to escape, several Methodist Christians went down to the beaches and preached the Good News to these would-be rafters. Their message was simple: If you get on that raft you confess faithlessness and hopelessness. But if you accept Jesus Christ at this moment and believe, you place your faith in the God of life, who has a purpose for you here in Cuba.

Many times people asked me, "Why do you come to Cuba at a time when most of us want to leave?" As the above-mentioned rafting crisis broke out, we had just completed our first term in Cuba and were faced with the decision of whether to continue in Cuba for a second term or return home. One close friend begged us not to return for the sake of our children. Nevertheless, we felt the hand of God guiding us to accompany the Cuban people during a difficult time. So many Cubans and foreigners had left during crucial times; Diana and I felt called to be faithful to our word and serve two full terms.

Three years later, when we completed our second term, I had accumulated enough service with the mission board to be eligible for a paid study leave. In addition, Diana and I wanted to have another child. But it was difficult to leave Cuba, as we felt welcome among the Cuban church and together had experienced so many life-changing events.

Nevertheless, in October of 1996, with tears in our eyes we informed the secretary for Latin America, German Acevedo, and the Cuban church of our intention to complete our service the following June. We began a series of goodbye parties in the seminary in Matanzas, Santa Fe Methodist Church (where Diana was appointed as pastor) and finally the annual conference.

On a personal level, we left behind many friends and colleagues that had become our family over the years. Our children also left behind many happy childhood memories. They still consider themselves "Cubans" because they spent the heart of their childhood years growing up in Cuba. On a professional level, we left with a sense of satisfaction as the two main projects that had begun under our leadership were well established. Cubans are so competent and able to run their own church and programs that they did not need missionaries to stay for a lengthy period.   With a waiting list of Volunteers in Missions teams ready to visit Cuba (see page 116) and a Cuban team of interpreters, we knew that our presence was no longer necessary.   Similarly, my wife had trained a group of Cuban youth to assume the leadership of the "Envianos" clown and puppet ministry.   On a much deeper spiritual level, we felt that the Cubans had given us much more than we could possibly offer and together we participated in the *Missio Dei*.   We were saddened to leave these friends and ministries, yet we departed following Annual Conference in June of 1997 with a sense of thanksgiving for all the wonderful experiences that God had bestowed upon us.

While I was able to leave with my family, the Methodist Church has stayed in Cuba throughout the difficult years of adversity and is accompanying the people, attempting to be God's instrument in the present day. When a people or a church are faithful to God's calling and open to the life-giving Spirit, just as the people called Methodists were three centuries ago, then God can give birth to an authentic revival. If the Cuban church embodies the God of life in the Cuban context, then it avails itself to be revived and used as a life-giving body.

If the revival is overwhelmed by foreign influences or practices, however, it can easily become subservient to foreign agendas and ceases to be a movement of God. Therefore it is the Cuban church that is called to be an instrument of God and point to signs of the kingdom in Cuba. Meanwhile, concerned friends abroad have the responsibility to show concrete gestures of solidarity— for example, prayer, direct assistance, and political activism in one's own country— to encourage the empowerment and self-determination for Cubans that all people deserve.

FOOTNOTES

195 Nancy R. Gibbs, "Dire Straits," *Time*, August 29, 1994, Vol.144, No.9, 28(5).
196 Ibid.

Bibliography

Alvarez, Carmelo, Cuba: *Testimonio Cristiano, Vivencia Revolucionaria.* San José, Costa Rica: DEI, 1990.

American Association for World Health, "The Impact of the U.S. Embargo on Health and Nutrition in Cuba," Washington, D.C., March, 1997.

Arce Martínez, Sergio, *The Church and Socialism: Reflections from a Cuban Context.* New York: Circus Publications, 1985.

Arias, Mortimer, "Methodist Societies in the Eighteenth Century and Christian Base Communities in the Twentieth Century," in Theodore Runyon, *Wesley Theology Today.* Nashville: Kingswood Books, 1985. p.236.

Background Notes, U.S. State Department, 1990.

Background Notes, U.S. State Department, 1993.

Baker's Dictionary of Theology, Grand Rapids, MI: Baker Book House, 1960.

Baloyra, Enrique A. & James A. Morris (eds.), *Conflict and Change in Cuba.* Albuquerque: New Mexico Press, 1993.

Benazet, Guido, *Una Paloma Blanca sobre una Isla Llamada Cuba.* Hialeah, FL: Editorial A White Dove, 1993.

Betto, Frei, *Fidel y La Religión.* La Habana: *Oficina de Publicaciones del Consejo de Estado,*1985.

Bibles International, "God's Time for Cuba," Window on the World, Vol.7, No.1, 1997.

Bilski, Andrew, "Damning the Flood," *Maclean's,* August 29, 1994, Vol.107, No.35, p.18.

Brenner, Philip and Saul Landau, "Passive Aggressive," *NACLA Report on the Americas,* Vol.24, No.3 (Nov., 1990), pp. 13-26.

Burgess, Stanley M. and Alexander Patrick (eds.), *Dictionary of Pentecostal and Charismatic Movements.* Grand Rapids, MI: Zondervan Publishing House, 1988.

Cepéda, Rafael, *La Herencia Misionera en Cuba.* San José, Costa Rica: DEI, 1986.

Chilcote, Paul W., *She Offered Them Christ*. Nashville: Abingdon Press, 1993.

Christianson, Larry, *A Charismatic Approach to Social Action*. Minneapolis: Bethany Fellowship, 1974.

Christophers, Samuel, *Class Meetings in Relation to the Design and Success of Methodism*. London: Wesleyan Conference Office, 1873.

"Con Dios y Con la Patria," encounter between leaders of the *Consejo Ecuménico de Cuba* and Fidel Castro, April 2, 1990, La Habana, Cuba.

Cox, Harvey, *Fire From Heaven*. Reading, MA: Addison-Wesley Publishing Company, 1995.

Conferencia de Obispos de la Iglesia Cat-lica en Cuba, "El Amor todo lo Espera," *La Voz de la Iglesia en Cuba*, México: Buena Prensa, S.A., 1995, pp.399-418.

Davies, Rupert E., *Methodism*. London: Epworth Press, 1985.

d'Epinay, Christian Lalive, *Haven of the Masses*. Santiago de Cuba: *Editorial del oli*,1968.

El Evangelista Cubano, *Tomo 59*, No.3, Dec., 1993, p.7.

Gibbs, Nancy R., "Dire Straits," *Time*, August 29, 1994, Vol.144, No.9, p.28.

Gomez Treto, Raul. *La Iglesia Católica durante la Construcción del Socialismo en Cuba*. Cuba: CEHILA, 1994.

Gunter, Stephen, *The Limits of Love Divine: John Wesley's Response to Antinomianism and Enthusiasm*. Nashville: Kingswood Books, 1989.

Heitzenrater, Richard, *Wesley and the People Called Methodists*. Nashville: Abingdon Press, 1995.

The Holy Bible, NRSV, Nashville: Thomas Nelson, Inc., 1989.

La Iglesia Metodista en Cuba, Disciplina de la Iglesia Metodista en Cuba. Conferencia General, March, 1991.

_____, "Sobre el Espiritu Santo," *La Conferencia Anual de La Iglesia Metodista en Cuba*, La Habana, Cuba, 1993.

_____, "Mensaje de la Conferencia Annual," *La Conferencia Annual de La Iglesia Metodista en Cuba*, La Habana, Cuba, 1993.

The Interpreter's Bible, Vol.6, Nashville: Abingdon Press, 1980.

Kohlenberger, John R.(ed.), *The NIV Interlinear Hebrew-English Old Testament, Vol.4*. Grand Rapids, MI: Zondervan Publishing House, 1979.

Jeffrey, Paul, "Cubans Continue to Survive Hardships," *Latinamerica Press*, (June 11, 1992), Vol.24, No.22, p.6.

_____, "Cuba: Changes and Challenges", *Response*, (April, 1992), pp.24-47.

Kennedy, John W., "Cuba"s Next Revolution", *Christianity Today*, Vol.42, No.1, (Jan., 12, 1998), pp.19-25.

Lopez Vigil, Maria, "*El Papa en Cuba: Brújula para Peregrinos*," *Envio*, A-o 16, No.188 (Nov., 1997), pp.11-22.

Malone, Shawn T., "Conflict, Coexistence, and Cooperation: Church-State Relations in Cuba," The Cuba Project, Center for Latin American Studies, Georgetown University, August, 1996.

Mesa-Lago, Carmelo (ed.), *Cuba after the Cold War*. Pittsburgh: Pittsburgh Press, 1993.

_____, *The Economy of Socialist Cuba*, Albuquerque: University of New Mexico Press, 1981.

Neblett, Sterling Augustus, *Methodism's First Fifty Years in Cuba*. Wilmore, KY: Asbury Press, 1976.

Outler, Albert, *Theology in the Wesleyan Spirit*. Nashville: Discipleship Resources, 1974.

_____ and Heitzenrater, Richard P., *John Wesley's Sermons: An Anthology*. Nashville: Abingdon, 1991

Pérez, Carlos, *Un Resumen de los Setenta Años de Labor de la Iglesia Metodista en Cuba 1898-1968*, Miami, FL: self-published, 1983.

Planas, J. Richard, "The Impact of Soviet Reforms on Cuban Socialism," *Conflict and Change in Cuba*. Enrique A. Baloyra and James A. Morris (eds.), Albuquerque: New Mexico Press, 1993, p.248.

Robbins, Carla Anne, "Civic Lessons: As Economy Struggles, Cubans Find a Crack in Castro's Control," *Wall Street Journal*, (June, 1995), Vol.76, No.172.

Rodríguez, Jr., Armando, "*Compartamos el Pan y el Vino: Análisis crítico de la Eucaristía en el pensamiento y la practica de la Iglesia Metodista en Cuba*," thesis, Matanzas, Cuba: Seminario Evangélico de Teologia, 1994.

Rohter, Larry, "Cuba's unwanted refugees: squatters in Havana," *New York Times*, October 20, 1997, Vol.147, No.293, p.A6.

Runyan, Theodore, *Sanctification & Liberation*. Nashville: Abingdon Press, 1981.

_____. (ed.), *What the Spirit Is Saying to the Churches*. New York: Hawthorne Books, 1975.

Ruffin, Patricia, *Capitalism and Socialism in Cuba: A Study of Dependency, Development and Underdevelopment*. New York: St. Martin's Press, 1990.

Santos Torres, Sergio, *"Bautismo de Jesus con el Espiritu Santo,"* thesis. Matanzas, Cuba: Seminario Evangelico de Teologia, 1997.

Shearman, Peter, *The Soviet Union and Cuba*. London: The Royal Institute of International Affairs, 1987.

Taylor, Clyde W., *Protestant Missions in Latin America: A Statistical Survey*. Washington: Evangelical Foreign Missions Association, 1961.

U.S. Congress, "Cuba in a changing world: the United States-Soviet-Cuba triangle," (hearings) April 30, July 11 and 31, 1991, iii, p.231.

Watson, David Lowes, *Covenant Discipleship*. Nashville: Discipleship Resources, 1989.

Webster's Intermediate Dictionary, Springfield, MA: Merriam-Webster Publishers, 1972.

Willis, Joseph, *The Class and the Congregation of Wesleyan Methodism*. London: Elliot Stock, 1869.

Wingeier-Rayo, Diana. *"La Presencia Femenina en los Ministerios de la Iglesia: un aporte crítico para la Iglesia Metodista en Cuba de la participacion de la mujer en la mision de la Iglesia,"* thesis, Matanzas, Cuba: Seminario Evangelico de Teologia, 1997.

_____, "Area Report of Cuba," Atlanta: Mission Resource Center, December, 1994.

Wingeier-Rayo, Philip, "One Who Stayed," *New World Outlook*, (Jan.-Feb., 1995), p.38.

_____, and Chilcote, Paul W., "The Wesleyan Revival and Methodism in Cuba," *Quarterly Review*, Vol.17, No.3 (Fall, 1997), pp.207-221.

The Works of John Wesley. Franklin, Tennessee: Providence House Publishers, 1995.

Zimbalist, Andrew (ed.), *Cuba's Socialist Economy Toward the 1990's*. London: Lynne Rienner Publishers, 1987.

INTERVIEWS

Ajo Fernandez, Joel, bishop emeritus of *La Iglesia Metodista en Cuba*, interview with Philip Wingeier-Rayo, Racine, Wisconsin, April 8, 1998.

Benazet, Guido, interview with Philip Wingeier-Rayo, Orlando, Florida, March 21, 1998.

González, Emilio, Cuban Methodist pastor, interview with Phil Wingeier-Rayo, Zolfo Springs, Florida, March 21, 1998.

Rankin, Larry, Conference Mission Secretary, telephone interview with Phil Wingeier-Rayo, Florida, Annual Conference, April 17, 1998.

Rodríguez, Sr., Armando, bishop emeritus of *La Iglesia Metodista en Cuba,* interview with Phil Wingeier-Rayo, Des Plaines, Illinois, January 20, 1998.

Rodríguez, Jr., Armando. Interview with Philip Wingeier-Rayo, Evanston, Illinois, March 17, 1998.

WEB SITES

www.Cubabloqueo.cu/leyes/cda.pdf

www.historyofcuba.com/history/funfacts/embargo.htm

www.umc.org/umns/story.asp

About the Author

Born to missionary parents in Singapore, Dr. Philip Wingeier-Rayo is a third-generation missionary. After completing his undergraduate degree at Earlham College in psychology and Spanish, he served as a Mission Intern of the General Board of Global Ministries of The United Methodist Church in Nicaragua and the Rio Grande Valley, Texas. Then he was selected by the GBGM to be assigned to Cuba, becoming the first Protestant missionary to enter Cuba in the Castro era.

He and his wife, Diana, a United Methodist pastor, served in Cuba from 1991-1997, and then another term in Mexico from 2000-2003, where she was appointed to a local church and he taught at the Methodist Seminary in Mexico City.

Dr. Wingeier earned his masters' degrees in theology from Garrett-Evangelical Theological Seminary and the Seminario Evangelico de Teologia in Matanzas, Cuba, and a Ph.D. from Chicago Theological Seminary. He is now Missionary-in-Residence at Pfeiffer University, organizing a new undergraduate degree in missions— the only program of its kind in the United Methodist Church.

The Wingeier-Rayos have three children, Massiel, Keffren and Isaiah (pictured above).